# Toddler Taming Tips

# Toddler Taming Tips

## A parent's guide to the first four years

## DR CHRISTOPHER GREEN

**Vermilion**
LONDON

1 3 5 7 9 10 8 6 4 2

First published in Australia and New Zealand in 2003 by
Doubleday
First published in the United Kingdom in 2003 by
Vermilion, an imprint of Ebury Press.
Random House UK Ltd.
Random House
20 Vauxhall Bridge Road
London SW1V 2SA

Random House Australia (Pty) Limited
20 Alfred Street, Milsons Point, Sydney,
New South Wales 2061, Australia

Random House New Zealand Limited
18 Poland Road, Glenfield,
Auckland 10, New Zealand

Random House (Pty) Limited
Endulini, 5A Jubilee Road, Parktown 2193, South Africa

Random House UK Limited Reg. No. 954009
www.randomhouse.co.uk
Papers used by Vermilion are natural, recyclable products
made from wood grown in sustainable forests.

A CIP catalogue record is available for this book from the
British Library

ISBN: 0091889677

Printed and bound in Denmark by
Nørhaven Paperback A/S, Viborg

# Contents

# Introduction

It is now 18 years since I first wrote *Toddler Taming* and the ideas are still relevant. I want to emphasise though that I have never 'tamed' a toddler.

*Toddler Taming Tips* still talks a lot about discipline. But discipline is not about punishment. It is about rewarding and encouraging: transmitting love and approval in your tone of voice; letting the little ones see the twinkle in your eye. On the whole I believe that discipline is a very positive thing. It is about expectations, empowerment, enjoyment and a sense of humour.

When I talk about expectations I mean that parents should know what is normal in children. It is important to realise that toddlers are not adults. This may seem obvious but some parents seem to make a big issue out of non-problems.

By empowerment I mean that raising children is entirely up to what feels right and works best for you.

Don't be brainwashed by other parents – what works for them may not necessarily be right for you and your child.

When I say enjoyment I mean to emphasise that toddlerhood is a wonderful time to be enjoyed. A lot of parents seem to spend their time coping, not enjoying, and this is not what you want. Don't miss the magic – it is only a few years of their life.

I cannot say enough about the importance of family. It is where we learn the ground rules: belonging, security and love.

Twenty-two years ago we left Belfast, Northern Ireland, with our two young children, to live in the most beautiful city in the world, Sydney, Australia. And the move brought great opportunities for us.

But I do have regrets.

While I was successful through my books, I regret that my boys were the most affected by the move to Australia. They were left with a wound that takes a long time to heal. What I am talking about is that they grew up away from their grandparents, aunts, uncles and cousins – the group of people that makes us feel secure and gives us a sense of belonging.

I also regret not spending more time with my own children. While I earned fame and fortune through writing my books and sharing the message, I feel I missed a lot of time with my family, the learning and the loving – the things that family is all about.

Time is something you can't repeat but if I had my time again, I would do things very differently.

This book is about parents spending their time understanding, savouring, seeing the magic, slowing down and bringing the fun back to parenting. And don't forget that sense of humour!

Christopher Green
Sydney 2003

# ONE

# What is a Toddler?

The toddler is an interesting little person, aged between 1 and 4 years. Some people call this stage the 'terrible twos', but it's not terrible – it's really a time of sweet innocence, dependence and a magic mind. Toddlers are built to a design that is perfect in every detail, but for one small defect – they have all the activity of an international airport, but the control tower doesn't work.

Toddlerhood starts at around the first birthday. At this age, little ones discover that they have the muscle to manipulate and challenge and are not backward about flexing it. Toddlerhood starts gradually with senseless and unthinking acts predominant up to the age of 1½ years, hits a peak at about 2 years and then gradually eases by 2½ years.

Some parents expect adult attitudes from their 2-year-olds, but at this age the 'sense centres' aren't yet on line.

**There would be fewer stressed parents if it were understood that these little people are not capable of adult logic.**

Parents who are unaware of this conduct deep and meaningful debates with their toddler. The child looks interested, but this is about as useful as discussing the good qualities of postmen with a Rottweiler.

At playgroup, parents are

embarrassed when their 2-year-old is rough with other children, grabs, bites and won't share things. There's no waiting at this stage. They interrupt, won't take turns and when they need a wee it has to be in 'this flowerpot'.

The toddler has no malice or aggression; his problem is simply caused by an underdeveloped control system. There's not a bad bone in these little bodies. It's easy for me to call these behaviours normal, but it's not so easy when parents are struggling at the battlefront. The antisocial toddler is criticised by experts who have never had children, or who've been fortunate enough to score an angel. Don't let others send you on a guilt trip – believe me, the most unsharing, shoving 2-year-old will turn into a polite, loving, grown-up.

During the toddler years, the aim is to steer them from trouble, savour the magic that they bring to new experiences and introduce adult attitudes when the child's brain is good and ready.

## What makes toddlers tick?

Whether you think of your bundle of joy as 'a little treasure', 'an ankle biter', 'a midget mafiosa', or 'the terrible 2-year-old', all toddlers have one thing in

# Toddlerhood – the goals

For the parents, toddlerhood is a time of:

- introducing controls
- guiding gently
- setting limits
- avoiding confrontation
- being 100 per cent firm when needed.

For the children, toddlerhood is all about:

- learning to control their bodies and behaviours
- toilet training
- controlling impulses – learning to wait
- learning that tantrums don't always mean they get their own way
- controlling frustration – learning a *little* patience
- being able to separate from parents
- sharing and realising that others also have rights.

common and that is an interesting collection of behavioural traits that are their trademark.

## Plenty of power

Small toddlers can exert an amazing amount of power over adults. If they don't get what they want, such is their protest that parents often buckle under the onslaught. Toddlerhood may be an age when children show little self-control but it doesn't stop them trying to control those around them.

It is not the power that causes the problem but rather how it is used. Toddlers are negative, show little sense and totally lack appreciation of the rights of others. With such a strong hand, all they have to do is dig in their heels and shout, and adults jump.

## Little sense

I'm going to be a bore and repeat this many times because knowing about sense is so important.

When people talk of the 'terrible twos' I believe it is really the 'terrible $1^1/_2$ to $2^1/_2$-year-olds' that they refer to. This short period is the time of minimum sense with maximum mobility.

**It is my belief that between the ages of 1 and 2 years most toddlers have zero sense. From this time on sense starts to grow with a significant amount present by 3 years.**

This is the age of unthinking behaviours (e.g. head-banging) and complete disregard for danger in the interests of the moment.

Young toddlers can argue, fight and get into no-win situations but they don't have the sense to know when to stop. For effective discipline, parents need to know when it is best to back down.

Some parents make very heavy weather of bringing up their children. They misread their toddler's behaviour and feel that the child is deliberately trying to upset them. They start believing their child is malicious – almost the enemy. They forget that having children is supposed to be fun.

Parents think they have a 'terrible two' but they are mostly just normal kids growing up.

## Wanting attention 25 hours a day

Toddlers love to be centre stage at all times. They want attention 24 hours a day and if you give this, then they will want 25 hours. Attention is important but it does take its toll. After a day of play, answering incessant questions and trying to keep one jump ahead of such inventive and imaginative little people, parents are exhausted. This is not physical exhaustion but a special sort of tiredness that leaves you numb from the neck upwards.

## Self-centredness

Most toddlers have tunnel vision, which focuses only on their own needs and happiness. When a child is playing and wants a particular toy, it is unlikely that he will ask politely for it. The idea of taking turns and thinking of another's point of view and sharing is quite foreign. Although young toddlers enjoy being with other children, they tend to play beside them rather than with them. This self-centred behaviour is normal for most toddlers.

## Ten-minute time frame

The young toddler lives only for the here and now. At this age praise and rewards must be immediate, while discipline must happen now or not at all. It is pointless punishing the 2-year-old hours after the event. It is equally foolish to expect the toddler to understand that being good today will be rewarded by going to the zoo next week.

## Toddler trademarks

Most toddlers:

- have more power than sense;

- want attention 25 hours a day;

- are self-centred; and

- live for the moment.

Parents should know this is normal, not blame themselves, then go with the flow.

# TWO

# Confident Parenting

Some years ago, when addressing a large gathering of good parents, I asked one simple question: 'How confident are you in your own parenting abilities?' Seventy-seven per cent of those who responded to this secret ballot said that they had serious doubts about what they were doing.

It seems that the more complicated child care theory becomes, the less we are prepared to trust our natural instincts. This leaves us vulnerable to a predictable group of factors that erode our confidence. Here are some things that get in the way.

## Not knowing what's normal

Often we feel we are the only ones with troubles when, if only we knew it, everyone else is in the same boat. With the toddler, some behavioural concerns are so common, they must be seen as a normal part of childhood. Remember, most toddlers have fiddly fingers, don't think of the future, have no sense, like constant attention, and often ignore much of what you say.

**Many behaviours would not be problems at all if only parents were more confident about what is normal toddler behaviour.**

It is said of normal 2-year-olds that 44 per cent attack their younger or older brother or sister, 50 per cent eat too little, 70 per cent resist going to bed, 83 per cent whinge and nag, 94 per cent constantly seek attention, 95 per cent are stubborn and 100 per cent are active and rarely still. Some children show these characteristics to a minor degree while others hold in their hand a full house.

There are enough genuine worries in the world without making ourselves feel inadequate by believing we are to blame for the normal non-problems of our toddlers.

## Ground down by competition

We live in a very competitive world and we can't help noticing how other people manage their homes, relationships and children. In the past, children spent most of their first six years at home, but now we parade them in public from their earliest days and with this comes competition and embarrassment.

As you wait in the baby clinic, you may wonder why all the other children seem bigger, stronger, toothier and more advanced than your meagre scrap. You love playgroup but you think that others watch you and

**Remember: slow down and see the magic.**

your children. At pre-school you may feel the pressure when your little one fails at cutting-out or romps around when the core of children are pasting, painting and listening to stories. Competitive parents tend to cloud the perspective by boasting about the rare and clever while keeping quiet about those common things, like bed wetting, that make us feel ashamed.

## Overwhelmed by experts

I often wonder if all child care experts were to be blown from the face of the earth, would parents be any the worse off. As I set out to demystify child care and boost confidence, it seems that a hundred others are out there hell bent on making it all much more difficult. Confidence is fragile enough without being confused by some of the way-out and incorrect ideas I hear, such as:

■ If both parents work it does harm to their children. *Not true*.

■ Dummies should never be used. *If they work, use them*.

■ Babies who fall asleep in their mother's arms will find it hard to settle themselves if they wake in the middle of the night. *If you love cuddling your baby to sleep and your baby loves being cuddled to sleep, then it's a bit of magic your baby should have.*

■ The toddler who wakes often every night must be comforted by its parent. *This is a sleep problem which should be cured quickly.*

■ The toddlers who play occasionally with their private parts do this as a sign of sexual abuse. *Nonsense. Little children do this because it feels pleasant and they are bored.*

Books full of impractical, out-of-touch ideas that set unattainably high goals, do nothing but generate fears and create feelings of parental inadequacy. These should be pulped and recycled to save some of the world's trees.

## Individuality counts

Every child is born an individual. One of the quickest ways to crush confidence is when parents try to force their children to be something they were never designed to be. The child with an active temperament will never sit still long enough to learn to read at the age of 3, any more than the gentle boy with the temperament of

St Francis will ever be suitable for the front row of the All Blacks rugby team.

We all have to learn to accept the child we have been given, and then do our best. Remember that as parents, we too are individuals, with our own temperaments and styles of parenting. We must have the confidence to do our own thing and not be brainwashed by those who do things differently.

## Hindrance from the helping professionals

Some professionals can make parents feel pretty inadequate. Even worse, some are still steeped in the prehistoric ideas of the 1950s and find it impossible to give any practical advice on behaviour without psychoanalysing the parents. Choose your professional well. The helping professions should be good at helping, but unfortunately this is not always the case.

Watch for the school of thought that says you should raise your children 'the one and only right way'. There is no one right way to bring up children. Child care fashions come and go while children look on bemused, showing how well they survive despite our professional interference.

# The foundation for happy, secure children

There is no doubt that our children thrive best when they:

■ *Are loved.* Everyone should feel loved and wanted.

■ *Are part of a family.* Do not underestimate the values of being close to grandparents, aunts, uncles and friends.

■ *Live in a stable, tension-free home.* Friction in adult relationships can never be hidden from children. The most considerate thing we as parents can do for our children is to be kinder to one another.

■ *Have parents who have reasonable expectations.* Unrealistic expectations cause non-problems that undermine parents unnecessarily.

■ *Are given a good adult example.* Children cannot behave better than those whose example they follow.

■ *Receive clear, consistent child care.* Children need to know where they stand and that what stands today will still be standing tomorrow.

- *Have fun and enjoyment in their lives.* Children should be brought up as apprentices to fun-loving parents **who enjoy having them around**.

# THREE

# Understanding Toddler Behaviour

There is an immense breadth of behaviour that can be confidently classed as normal. There is also great variation from family to family. When it comes to what is tolerable, I am in no doubt that this decision is in the eye of the beholder.

If you put a busy, noisy toddler in with a busy, noisy family, he will not be noticed, whilst a quiet, violin-playing, well-mannered child would stand out like a vegetarian at a butcher's picnic.

Tolerance depends on the individual make-up of the parents and how the world is treating us. It varies from day to day. When life is going well we can take a lot but on those bad days, a little toddlerhood goes a very long way.

As your tired brain becomes more tired, it may be easy to believe that your little one is in fact the enemy, out to get you. But I can assure you it is not like that. In reality he is just a toddler with absolutely no sense.

**Toddler behaviour is a worry to most parents, whether they are psychologists, plumbers, IT experts or paediatricians.**

From my experience, it appears that almost all behavioural concerns stem from a handful of triggers. Recognising these triggers can help you deal with the behaviour that follows.

# The 7 causes of toddler behaviours

When we parents are having a bad day, our toddlers' repertoire of behaviour may seem extensive but in fact almost every performance comes from one of seven very predictable origins. Awareness of these brings all behaviours into perspective and allows you to achieve a firm foundation for effective discipline. These behaviours are:

## 1. Attention seeking

Toddlers crave attention. If they can't get it by fair means they lower their sights, irritate their parents and grab it by some annoying act. This is by far the most common cause of toddler problems.

When a little child performs some particularly anti-social act, stand back and ask yourself why. *'If I was doing what that little terror is doing, what percentage would there be in it for me?'* For toddlers, the answer is nearly always the same: *'to gain attention'.*

## 2. Jealousy and competition

Jealousy and competition can bring problems for parents and arise from some quite predictable situations such as the arrival of a new baby, a visiting child, a long

# Grades of attention

Attention is deceptive. It comes in many grades and guises. If we visualise attention as a spectrum, graded from A to Z, we see two colourful extremes with many shades in between. Our children will usually aim for the best level of attention they can get, and if the best is not on offer they will descend through the grades until they find one that gives them what they want. Here are some examples:

- Grade A (the best) includes all those close parent–child interactions like talking, reading books, playing together and cuddling.

- If parents have their hands full and Grade A attention is not on offer, toddlers will drop down a grade or two to B, C or D. They will probably start asking endless questions, although they are clearly not in the slightest bit interested in the answers. At least it keeps the lines of communication open and gives them some reasonable attention.

- If Grades B, C or D don't work, a bit of arguing and debating is often seen as good value.

- Down in mid-alphabet, toddlers find that saying 'No' to everything will get Mum's undivided attention. If this, by some mischance, doesn't work, they can always climb on top of the baby or do unspeakable things to the cat, which is bound to stir up lots of attention.

- Further into the lower levels of the alphabet we'll find tantrums, breath-holding and even vomiting on demand. The payoff for toddlers may be a long way from Grade A but when top quality attention is not on offer it is still worth the effort.

session on the phone or even a quick chat with a friend when you are out shopping.

At around 2 years, little children are not richly endowed with values of sharing and seeing the other person's point of view. They like to be the star of the show no matter what and can be pretty antisocial when others step into their limelight. Time will soon cure this behaviour. Six more months can make all the difference.

## 3. Frustration

Tiny toddlers have ideas way above their abilities and when things don't go as they have planned they can become mighty frustrated. As parents we should accept that a certain amount of grizzling and tantrum throwing is due to frustration and not just bad behaviour. The toddler is trying to come to terms with the limitations of his abilities and at this time it is a cuddle and encouragement he needs, not punishment.

## 4. Fear of separation

Toddlers usually want to be close to their parents and get upset when separated. This is a normal stage of development and not a sign of sickness or bad behaviour. Anxiety over separation starts at about 7 months of age, intensifies to a peak just after the first birthday, and gradually wanes over the next three years. Their protest is not naughtiness, they are just telling you that you are important and they would prefer to stay close to you. Usually this can be overcome gradually with gentleness, not scolding and punishment.

## 5. Reaction to illness, tiredness, or emotional upset

When toddlers are sick, teething or have a temperature it is unreasonable to expect them to behave well. They feel uncomfortable and irritable, so why shouldn't they grizzle, dig in their heels and make a big drama out of life's trivial events. In times of sickness, it is best to accept all this as inevitable, then freewheel for a while, establishing a firm hold again once they are better.

When the home is unsettled and routines disturbed, behaviour may also take a turn for the worse. Starting work, moving house, new babies, visitors, late nights, holiday travel and family fights can all cause upsets. With changes and turmoil, expect a little bad behaviour and work on the cause of the tension rather than combating it with the stir of punitive discipline.

## 6. Unreal parental expectations

If parents expect a toddler to have adult values they are in for trouble. Toddlers have little sense, live for the here and now and certainly do not behave like grown-ups. They understand nothing of adult values, especially when it comes to expense, money, ownership and tact. Trying to make them grow up before their time is painful, pointless and a common cause of friction.

## 7. Behavioural beat-ups

Parents bring problems on themselves by taking an unimportant event and beating it into a great drama.

Both parents and toddlers can be very stubborn, but only mums and dads have the age and experience to know when it's best to back off.

Try to muster all your insight and intelligence to see when you are causing harm and not helping a situation. It takes two to develop a behavioural beat-up and as 50 per cent of the combatants, we parents should aim for peace and a quick and fair solution.

## Sensible expectations

It is upsetting that so few parents have any idea what constitutes normal toddler behaviour. We spend much of our lives feeling guilty, inadequate, self-recriminating and believing we are the only ones who cannot control our children. Life is tough enough without immobilising ourselves with such ill-founded guilt.

### All toddlers ...

- crave attention and hate to be ignored. Some are quite satisfied with their parents' best efforts, others would grumble unless 25 hours a day, 8 days a week were devoted solely to their care.

■ separate poorly from their caretakers. In the first three years a toddler prefers to play near his mother and does not like to let her out of his sight for long. For most, an unfamiliar child-minder causes initial problems, while being locked in a room or separated when out shopping is a major trauma.

■ tend to be busy little people. Some are extremely active and hardly ever still; others are just 'active'.

■ have little road sense or in fact little sense of danger. They are impulsive and unpredictable which is a hazard even in the apparently sensible child. All toddlers need close parental protection.

■ show little respect for other people's property. Their fingers are drawn as if by magnetism to everything they pass. Ornaments are broken and cupboards rearranged. Those ten active little digits have an amazing power to spread a sticky, jam-like substance over every surface they meet.

■ tend to be stubborn and wilful. Some are quite militant but others will bend to reason.

■ tend to be blind to the mountain of mess they generate. The tidy toddler who is neat and even picks up his own toys is the exception rather than the rule.

■ ask endless questions, the same one being repeated again and again, with little interest in the answer. This especially applies to the over-threes.

■ change their minds every minute. Are you going mad? No, this is just brainwashing, toddler style.

■ constantly interrupt adults. It is not that they want to be rude, but they believe that what they have got to contribute is much more important than the irrelevant ramblings of their parents.

■ make their parents feel inferior. Little children have an incredible ability to demoralise their parents. Many will act as complete angels when in the care of others, reserving their demonic side exclusively for their parents.

■ are extremely sensitive to upset, excitement and tension in their environment. Their sound sleep pattern can be upset by illness, holidays or stress. A minor alteration to the environment can often make the child who was fully toilet trained start to leak.

## Many toddlers . . .

- will sit and concentrate briefly to draw, do puzzles or attend to pre-reading tasks. A minority will settle for a long time but most become restless in about five minutes and look for a means of escape. Quite a large proportion of active little children will not sit even for the shortest period.

- are cuddly, affectionate, 'giving' children. There is, however, a minority who resent handling, are distant and seem to give a poor return of love to their parents.

- are determined and independent. Some become so belligerent that they refuse to be fed or dressed, even though they are far too young to do either task unaided. Other toddlers are passive, dependent and quite happy to be pampered and directed.

- are compulsive climbers. At an early age they will organise an expedition to the summit of the settee and once this has been scaled, will set out to conquer the benchtops, tables and anything that happens to be there. Other toddlers are more sensible and have a healthy fear of the 'painful stop at the end of the drop'.

■ go off their food around their first birthday, a proper eating pattern not returning for anything up to a year. Some will tolerate a narrow, unimaginative diet; others will eat anything in sight. Some eat main meals; others were born to be snackers.

■ have fears. Dogs, loud noises, new situations and strange objects and people cause distress in over half of this age group.

■ display a multitude of irritating habits. This of course is not only a problem with children.

■ have behaviour which fluctuates considerably from day to day and week to week. Bad days are usually blamed on teething, lack of sleep or 'something they ate'. These all make good scapegoats but it never seems to occur to parents that adults can have good days and bad days and we don't blame this on teething.

# FOUR

# Discipline

Every one of us, whether school child, toddler or adult, needs discipline. We all feel much happier and more secure when we have a disciplined lifestyle and know exactly where we stand. Children are happiest when they know that their parents are united, consistent and concerned enough to care how they behave.

Bringing up children may be no game but it will be more peaceful if all the players know the rules and have no doubt that the referee is both fair and in control.

## What is discipline?

When the word discipline is used many parents become flustered because they associate it with punishment but this is not what it is all about. Discipline is a far more attractive concept when viewed as a learning experience for our children rather than one of pain and punishment.

Discipline can be imposed on us from outside or it can come from within as self-discipline. Obviously young toddlers have no idea of self-discipline and at this tender age all direction must come externally from us, the parents. By pre-school age, children are ready to start taking some responsibility for their own affairs and this process can be helped if we loosen the reins and allow a little freedom of choice. This lets them feel the repercussions of their right and wrong decisions. The ultimate aim is to have self-discipline firmly established by the time they up and leave home.

## When to start

Babies in the first year certainly do not need discipline. They need love, routine and closeness. Toddlers, however, are completely different little people. They are at that interesting stage when they flex their muscles and challenge all around them. They most certainly need discipline, the amount of which depends on the temperament of the individual child and the tolerance of the parents.

Starting discipline is a very individual decision but the main message is to go gently at the beginning. Before the age of 2 our children do little which is devious, aggressive or nasty. Their actions just lack thought. Gentle firm guidance is usually sufficient, leaving the wrath-of-God-descend-ing-like-a-thunderbolt firmly in reserve.

**Parents should have sensible expectations of their toddler. No 2-year-old is going to think or behave like an adult.**

# Making life easier for yourself

Our children's behaviour depends on two competing factors: their God-given temperament and the environment they inhabit. This knowledge puts a lot of responsibility on us, the parents. While we are stuck with their temperament, environment is something we can always modify as we try to handle day to day situations better.

Here are some extremely simple ideas which we can all use to make life easier. Although most of these will be known, it is an unfortunate truth that when we are in a tired and demoralised state, commonsense is not too common.

■ Stay one step ahead and try to remain calm.

■ Don't nitpick, avoid escalation, accept the inevitable and once finished, forget it.

■ Both parents need to keep discipline consistent.

■ Give your toddler structure, routine and clear limits.

■ Have realistic expectations of your toddler's behaviour and avoid the triggers that set off bad behaviour (*see* Chapter 3).

■ Toddler-proof your home (*see* Chapter 6).

■ Avoid battles that cannot be won.

■ When all else fails get outside.

## Behaviour – discipline questions

A vast majority of behaviours which concern parents are really non-problems which would not arise if we had more enlightened expectations of our little ones. Here are some questions which are best answered with understanding, not discipline:

■ *'If I say no, he whinges until I give in.'*
Little children are extremely clever at getting what they want from their parents. Some have developed whingeing into an art form, which so grates on their parents' nerves, that the most convincing 'No!' can be turned to a 'Yes' with only two minutes of torture. Was the issue worth fighting over?

■ *No* – next time don't rise to trivial triggers.

■ *Yes* – be firm, consistent and convincing. Don't ever give in to the whinge. Divert. Move away.

# Tidying up toys

Some children seem to be born tidy, while others are quite oblivious to the disaster area they inhabit. The former are easily trained to be neat, the latter will pose a problem, but things can always be improved and made easier:

■ Have sensible expectations. Cleanliness and tidiness are possible but not usual in the under 3-year-old.

■ Restrict the number of toys on offer. Little children don't need an entire warehouse full of playthings. Put some away, then rotate and reintroduce bringing new interest in forgotten toys.

■ Avoid any product which comes apart into twenty tiny pieces. If you don't you will write off weeks of your life, looking for the lost bits.

■ Have a big cardboard box for toys and try to establish a habit which encourages it to be filled at the end of play.

■ Give a positive statement that it is time to tidy. Softly reward their efforts to help with appreciation. Then move on to some rewarding activity.

■ *'My 2-year-old screams and pushes if any visiting child dares touch his toys.'*
Young toddlers are not good at socialisation and sharing. They believe they are important people, they know that the toy is theirs, so they expect all intruders to keep their hands well clear. At this young age they need gentle guidance, after which time and maturity will bring about some major miracles.

■ Briefly mention the expectation to share. Don't force the issue, don't make a scene.

■ Compensate the empty-handed visitor with the majority share of attention.

■ Introduce another area of entertainment to distract. Time Out is not appropriate here, unless there is a repeated heavy assault on the visitor.

## Non-problems need no discipline

■ *'I tried your behaviour techniques but they made things worse, not better.'*
When children find their old antics don't get results, they have to switch up the volume, which is generally the sign that you are starting to get through. Stick at it for success.

■ **'How do I take comforters and cuddly toys from my toddler?'**
Why should you take comfort from a toddler? Some parents prise thumbs, pacifiers, cuddly toys and comforters away from children at the youngest age to promote independence. We all need our comforters; why rush children and rob them of their childhood.

■ **'When I put him to bed he immediately asks for a drink, a wee wee, a brighter light, etc.'**
Many children procrastinate at bedtime in an attempt to keep those they love close as long as possible. Give lots of attention before you put them down, then be decisive, firm and go.

■ **'My 2-year-old seems to want snacks all the time and does not eat big amounts at mealtimes.'**
Toddlers eat when they are hungry and are not governed by our artificial adult mealtimes. Healthy snacks can provide excellent nutrition. If they are thriving, healthy and energetic, with a reasonable diet – relax.

# FIVE

# Discipline Techniques

Discipline is not about punishment, it's about encouraging, rewarding and moulding the child to behave in the correct way. On the whole, discipline is a very positive thing.

A behaviour which pays off for the child will generally be repeated, so what we want to make sure of is that the pay-off comes for the right behaviours, not the wrong ones.

## It's all in the voice

The best way to discipline a toddler is through your tone of voice. 'Good boy', 'Good girl', 'That's right', 'Well done', all that sort of thing, coupled with the way you look at your child when you say it. Transmit love and approval in your eyes. Let them see the twinkle in your eye. It's these kinds of tones and actions that we should mainly use to encourage the behaviours we want from our children.

When they aren't behaving the way you would like them to, use a firmer tone, a tone of disapproval, with a deadpan look on your face, and they will instinctively know that they have done something wrong. They may not understand what, but they know you are not pleased. You move away from them, signifying that they have done something you don't like and you don't want to be a part of it. In this way you are subtly moulding their behaviour.

# The six top tips of discipline

Here are some practical ways in which you can discipline your child without having to resort to the 'go to your room this instant!' method.

## I. Don't reward bad behaviour

Attention is the greatest reward of all and most of the attention we give to our children is subtle. Cut off the attention when things aren't going well and you don't want that behaviour repeated. You want them to know that you're not pleased. Watch out for the trap however. If the greatest reward is attention, and the greatest punishment is no attention, be aware that shouting at them, arguing with them or even smacking them qualifies as attention. Better to cut the attention off altogether.

## 2. Don't analyse your child's behaviour

Don't try looking for logic in it, because you won't find any. There's no point saying 'He's deliberately doing that to annoy me', because the chances are he isn't doing anything of the sort. He's just not thinking too much about what he is doing. 'He's deliberately disobeying me,' you say. It's not disobedience he just has a very short attention span.

Parents can get themselves into a lot of trouble in this way, grounding their 2-year-olds for long periods of time for alleged disobedience. It's to no avail. The debate about good and evil is an utter waste of time at this age. Leave it until they're over 5.

## 3. Diversion is your greatest weapon

All little children are very easily diverted, so when a child is about to embark on some form of behaviour of which you disapprove, you can say something like: 'Look, there's a dog in the garden, oh, it's gone round the corner.' This often works. It may be dishonest, but it can save your sanity!

## 4. Know the triggers

I bet you know all the ways to have an absolutely rotten day with your child. There are certain things that are guaranteed to wind your child up – for example, going to the supermarket. So if you know the situations which trigger off bad behaviour in your child, then avoid them at this early age.

## 5. Give clear instructions

Clear communication is one of the tricks of positive parenting. It isn't a matter of saying to your child 'Would you like to pick your toys up now?' but rather looking the child straight in the eye and saying 'John, pick up your toys. Here, I'll give you a hand.' Toddlers play you like a poker machine. They try you out, because they know that if they play for long enough you will eventually give in and they win the jackpot. Well, the trick is never to allow the jackpot to be won.

## 6. Ignore the unimportant

So many parents nitpick over all sorts of irrelevant stuff, wind themselves up like cuckoo clocks and get the children so stirred up that they behave really badly. The trick is to concentrate on the 20 per cent that really matters and ignore the 80 per cent that is irrelevant. This is important. Don't forget, however, that when you are choosing to ignore certain behaviours which you may not like, do it firmly but calmly, cut off your attention and don't get drawn in to what's happening.

# Diversion

Diversion is one of those good old-fashioned remedies that has stood the test of time and still comes out with flying colours.

Think back some years to when you were at granny's, just about to deleaf her pot plants like a dose of Agent Orange. She says quietly, 'I just remembered I have those lollies in the big jar in the kitchen'. With this your hands disengaged from the plant and you were off to the kitchen with the speed of Phar Lap from the gate. With all this never a voice was raised, peace was restored and the plant continued to do its bit to combat the greenhouse effect.

Today's parents can use the same technique with equal success. It is particularly useful with younger children. When it seems you are about to run headlong into a bit of bother, it is often easier to quickly divert the child's attention before the obnoxious behaviour has time to take hold. There is an exact psychological moment that the clever parent can sense and if grasped, the situation is saved before control has been lost.

# Encourage the good, discourage the bad

Behaviour modification simply states that any behaviour that is reinforced by rewards will tend to be repeated, and any behaviour that is not noticed, encouraged and reinforced will probably disappear.

In young children behaviour modification will work best if the good behaviour is rewarded quickly. Even a minute after the event the reward will have lost some of its power at this age. The technique must be used consistently if it is going to be effective. If a behaviour is going to be ignored and underplayed this must happen five out of every five times it occurs. If the ignoring is restricted to four out of five occurrences it will always be worth trying you out.

# What is a reward?

In behaviour work there are two styles of rewards. There are the soft or social rewards and then there are those which are hard and tangible.

## Soft or social rewards

These refer to giving attention, praise, smiles and touch. Of these, attention is the main reinforcer and when used wisely it can be very powerful. When misused, however, it can promote some mighty unwelcome behaviours. Both children and adults are very sensitive to soft, subtle boosting of behaviour techniques such as being noticed, or by the warmth of your voice, or that twinkle in your eye.

## Hard rewards

These are the more tangible items like a smiley stamp, a gold star on a chart, a 'Thomas the Tank Engine' sticker, or a host of little toys. Then there are all those sweet rewards that tend to turn both your child's teeth and the dentist's bank balance black.

## Soft or hard rewards

When deciding whether to use soft or hard rewards, the child's age is an important factor. Most toddlers are very happy with soft rewards, particularly attention, whilst older children are more aware of the value of objects and may do better with hard rewards, especially those that jingle in the pocket.

## Rewards and bribery

There is a very subtle difference between reward and bribery. A bribe is seen as a form of blackmail, where the child is told that he can only have something after he has performed a certain task. The behaviour modification reward comes as an immediate and unannounced bonus after the good behaviour has appeared. Very often the difference between bribes and rewards is far from clear and though I would prefer rewards, if a bit of good old-fashioned bribery achieves the desired effect, then go for it.

## Getting it back to front

Behaviour modification techniques allow us to steer a stubborn toddler around trouble without becoming drawn into any futile fights. However, it does have one great weakness. It is far too easy to get back to front. The technique has no safety lock which makes it boost only the good.

Many times we may unknowingly get it so reversed that it becomes an enemy, not an ally. A common example of getting it back to front would be with feeding. You put food in front of the toddler, he takes one look at it, and says 'yuk!'. Immediately the adults start to act like toddlers. Mum makes aeroplane noises, dad juggles oranges and the dog probably performs circus tricks. With so much reward for not eating, the mouth remains shut, tight as a Scotsman's purse. Now you have created a feeding problem.

Start again. He looks at the food: 'Yuk!' You ignore this. He either eats or ends up with hunger pains, but you maintain your sanity and have no future fights over food.

## Time Out

When all your best discipline has been tried and is getting you nowhere, when you are rapidly losing control and your little one knows it – don't snap, don't smack, use Time Out. Once you shout, argue, become irrational and behave like a toddler, the game is lost.

The aim of Time Out is to remove the child from a deteriorating or stalemate situation and place him, for a short time, in another room. This takes the child from his position on centre stage to a less prominent place, where his antics pass unnoticed. He has time to cool off and this also permits the parents to calm down.

Time Out is a powerful method of maintaining peace in the home and if used properly, reduces a lot of emotional tension without frightening or upsetting the child. As the tension settles and the child understands clearly the limits placed on him, this leads to a closer and happier life for all.

Real parents with difficult children do have their breaking point and it is never smart to see how close you can get to this very dangerous situation. When losing control, use Time Out.

## Is there a place for democracy?

An amazing amount of parental energy is consumed each day, arguing, debating and being democratic with little children. Three- to 4-year-old toddlers love attention and one of the main ploys to guarantee a constant flow of this commodity is to ask endless questions. When you examine what is asked, you will find that their range is remarkably small, little interest is shown in the answers and the same question is repeated again and again, as long as we parents rise to the bait.

Now, to ask lots of questions is a rather quaint characteristic and should be encouraged up to a point, but when debating, questioning and arguing goes on and on, bearing no relationship to the quest for knowledge, that is a different matter. When this verbal ping pong starts, parents must ask themselves *'Is this getting us anywhere or is the real reason for the exercise to stir us up?'*. Educate and listen to little people but when the sole object of the exercise is to wind you up – drop democracy.

# Smacking

Smacking is a sensitive subject with a whole army of people lined up on both sides of the argument. Whether it is a good or bad way to treat children, it is a fact of life that some parents will smack their children.

In the big picture of things, the occasional corrective smack is pretty harmless, though it still remains an ineffective form of discipline. It usually falls flat because it has been doled out in a fit of temper, following which our little ones capitalise on all our guilt and weaknesses and use them to their own advantage.

**Smacking is a poor form of discipline, but it is used by some parents in real life.**

If you have to resort to smacking your toddler, then you might as well have some idea of the possible outcomes – good and bad.

## Smacking – the rights . . .

■ *Resolves a stalemate situation*
Smacking is useful when toddlers and parents find themselves locked in a hopeless stalemate situation over some issue that must be seen through to the end, for example, if a child refuses to stay buckled up

in the car seat. When all else has failed and our authority is on the line a gentle smack will usually bring resolution within minutes.

■ *Deterrent to danger*
I believe that smacking may be a worthwhile deterrent to ensure that a dangerous life-threatening act is never repeated. I see nothing wrong with giving an immediate smack which will strongly reinforce the message that whatever has just taken place must never happen again. Cats may have nine lives, but this does not extend to children. Even if a painful smack did produce minor emotional trauma, this must be a small price to pay if it prevents the major pain of injury and keeps our children alive and healthy.

## ...and wrongs
■ *Smacking not followed through*
Most smacks seem to descend when parents are angry. This may make them feel better at the time, but it is often ill-aimed discipline, both badly timed and inappropriate. The problem for most parents comes about two minutes later, when, after the child's flood of tears, anger turns to guilt. The guilty parent cuddles the child, the punishment turns into

a reward and then the game is lost. For some parents, a quick smack may diffuse a situation and give back control, but unless it is followed through properly it is all too easy to blow it.

- *The last straw smack*
  Most of the smacks parents dole out are at times when they have had a gutful and can take no more. Often the smack arrives after a long series of annoyances and is precipitated by some trivial event which becomes the last straw that breaks the parent's back. This certainly releases a lot of anger for the parent, but it tends to confuse the child.

Be it good or bad, smacking is a form of discipline that continues to be used by many good, loving parents. It certainly has an effect on a child with a fairly easy-going temperament, though I believe that there are far better forms of discipline for these children.

Parents with a difficult child need all the means of discipline they can muster. However, when discipline is most needed, smacking becomes both ineffective and dangerous. Desperate parents resort to a smack, and when that fails, they smack harder. Anger, resentment and loss of control can set in and the potential for abuse may not be far off.

# SIX

# Toddler Proofing Your Life

Life can be made so much easier if you live in a suitably fortified home. Child proofing becomes a necessity just after the first birthday when the toddler is becoming extremely inquisitive and much more mobile, with sense at a standstill. I have seen some parents take child proofing so seriously that they crawled around the house on their hands and knees doing a trouble shooting survey from toddler level. This is a bit over the top but however you do it, toddler proofing is important.

## Fiddly fingers and the collapse of the dream home

When newly weds move into their first home they love to display their prize possessions, usually at toddler height. It comes as a rude shock when a little terror bursts on the scene and starts fingering the ornaments and taking the house apart. Now a major rethink is called for.

**If you have a fast-moving, inquisitive toddler, child proofing is not just advisable, it is a necessity.**

Sure you can leave those tempting trinkets lying around and if you say no and divert enough, he will eventually learn not to touch them, but it is rarely worth the hassle. Sensible parents keep temptation out of toddlers' way, gradually reintroducing things several years down the track.

## Latches, locks and prohibited areas

Keep breakables in a child proof cupboard or up high on a shelf. If you have good furniture in a good room with a snow white carpet, it is often best to declare this out of bounds. If your teaspoons are flushed down the toilet – put a latch on the cutlery drawer. Some cupboards will need to be latched and out of bounds, while others are open to play in and explore. Cupboards with saucepans, vegetables and thick-skin fruit are always popular and safer, while those with sharp knives, detergents and drain cleaners are an absolute no-no.

## Make-up and indelible markers

Many toddlers have wonderful artistic talents, particularly when it comes to finger painting on bench tops, the floor or mirrors. Lipstick, nail polish, make-up creams and indelible markers should be kept well out of reach. Any pen with ink that is not easily and instantly washable must be kept under the tightest security.

## Dangers, dogs and sharp edges

Houses with glass doors or windows that come down to floor level pose a danger to the child. If he falls through the glass he will suffer severe cuts and even greater injury if he rides his tricycle through an unprotected first floor window to the ground below. Block such dangers with furniture, fit temporary bars across the window and use safety glass where possible.

Safety plugs should be fitted over power points as young children have the sort of fascination with electricity that a fly has with a zapper. It is essential to have a commercial circuit-breaker fitted to your junction box outside, and then at least you can rest safe in the knowledge that even if he does poke a knife into the electric toaster he should survive to poke another day.

Furniture and household items with sharp edges that are likely to cut or damage either him or something else are best removed altogether or a soft material can be taped over them.

It is imperative that all medicines are stored safely in a securely locked cupboard high up out of harm's way. It is a common mistake for people who are very conscientious about storing medicines to leave even more dangerous products within easy reach in the kitchen, laundry or garden shed. Bleach, rat poison, weed killer, drain cleaner and dishwashing detergent are the sort of offenders that must be locked well away.

Pets and toddlers generally mix well but there is no place in the same house for a savage dog who bites when teased, however important his role as a guard dog may seem.

**It is important to toddler proof your home for your child's safety, the security of your belongings and your own peace of mind.**

## Fortify the compound

Coping with an active toddler is always easier if you have access to a secure garden. They need the space but you can never relax unless there are fences and gates to prevent escape onto the road.

Where fencing is inadequate and roads are busy, all doors leading from the house must be immobilised. The best methods are a high-level latch, security chain or deadlock. If you have one of those quiet, angelic, predictable children or are surrounded by acres of gently rolling parkland sweeping majestically to the horizon, this will all seem a bit unnecessary.

## The playpen

And finally, the playpen. It seems a marvellous invention for keeping active children out of mischief. Although sound in theory, it rarely works in practice, because extremely active children need space and protest if put in a playpen. Some parents say that the playpen is for their own use. They place a comfortable chair inside it, then sit back and read a book while the child runs around the house.

For a complete home safety checklist, *see* Appendix I.

# SEVEN

# Tantrums

Tantrums are the trademark of the toddler. They start around the first birthday, but generally by the age of 4, most children have learnt that there are better ways to get what they want.

In the hands of the skilful toddler a tantrum is an art form which can be brought about by a number of different stimuli. Not all tantrums are caused simply by a parent thwarting a wilful child in mid-activity. Some come from the inner frustrations of the toddler himself, who is being stirred up, or is impatient with his lack of ability.

## Treating the tantrum

The treatment of the tantrum depends on the age of the child, the reason for the behaviour and where the performance is being staged (in the home or outside).

In the first year of toddlerhood, before the second birthday, behaviour often just happens, without much thought or reason. Where possible at this age it is best to guide and be gentle. This can be the case throughout toddlerhood; however it is different when you have a 3-year-old who uses a tantrum to openly defy his parents' authority. This is absolutely not on. When authority is challenged, the parents must be consistent and stand firm.

*Some toddlers play their parents like poker machines*. If their efforts still score jackpots, then they will continue to play. If parents review their discipline and rig the odds so the toddlers never win, they may crank away but all to no avail. At this point even a 2-year-old should see that it is just not worth the effort.

*If a young one becomes frustrated* and throws tantrums because he has plans and designs which are way ahead of his technical ability, then it is not punishment he needs but a helping hand and comfort. Any child who is sick or in a home which is upset needs the gentle approach.

## Tackling tantrums in the home

Tackling tantrums is easy in theory but never quite as simple in practice. Here's one scenario with some universal tips to help see you through:

■ The 2½-year-old music lover decides he wants to fiddle with big sister's Walkman. This is not wise; you take it gently from him and place it safely on a high shelf.

■ Explain calmly, clearly and in three words or less why he can't have it. He is not satisfied with the situation.

■ He ignites his engines and they start to rev up in preparation for take-off. This is a good time to divert his attention. 'Here is Dad home early,' you say as you look out the window. 'Oh no, it was another white Ford.'

■ This hasn't worked, he is now revved up almost to full thrust. Now a tantrum is inevitable – CRASH! – he hits the deck, arms and legs going with all the grunts, groans, hype and genuine hurt of a professional wrestler.

■ Now even the most serene and best adjusted parents are severely stressed. Hands tremble, palms are sweaty, blood pressure has surged, you are close to having a stroke.

■ This is the time you should ignore, but this is not easy. Luckily it is sufficient to pretend to ignore.

■ Stay calm, don't fuss, don't notice, don't argue, go about your business.

■ Move away to a different room. Wash the dishes, peel the vegies, hang out the laundry, get outside for a breath of air.

*Note: Now think for a moment what is going on in the mind of a tantrum-throwing toddler. Here he is having put on his best Oscar-winning performance and in mid-act the audience has upped and walked out. With most actors if this happened, they would stop there and then, but of course they are not toddlers.*

■ Now that the audience has moved away and is ignoring him, the faint-hearted toddler gives up, waves the white flag and with a sniff and sob, goes for comfort. If this happens forgive, forget, don't lecture, be gentle. Don't be over-effusive; after all the victory was the parent's and the tantrum must not gain a great reward.

■ Meanwhile, back on the lounge-room carpet, the militant is still in full flight. 'This is a bit off,' he thinks, stomping out after mum and putting on twice the tantrum at mum's feet.

■ The volume is now rising, your heels are being kicked and you are rapidly losing your grip. Don't forget that we parents are the big people who should stay in control and in charge. While still on top use Time Out.

- Lift the little one gently, without anger or hate, and put him firmly and decisively in his room. Do this with complete conviction, leaving him in no doubt that you are 100 per cent serious.

- As you leave, say very firmly, in few words, that he must stay until in complete control, then extract yourself rapidly to a distant part of the house.

- Whether he comes out in one minute or in fifteen, the time is irrelevant, as long as the tension has eased and the unwinnable confrontation has passed.

- Forgive, don't point score, don't hold a grudge and get him moving along to some new and interesting activity. Loosen up and leave the tantrum and tension in the past.

## The supermarket special

Tantrums are not usually difficult to manage when at home but are a different matter when thrown in some prominent public place. What is worse, whatever you do, half the people watching will think it is wrong.

Many parents find shopping stressful and may even feel ashamed when they are out in public, convinced they are failures who can't control their children. Don't be fooled. While you are being embarrassed in public, crowds of similar children are left with a neighbour, casual care, or maybe even in a heavily fortified dungeon at grandma's place.

**If shopping and your toddler don't mix, use grandparents, a neighbour or occasional care, to allow tantrum-free shopping.**

If you do have the supermarket anarchist on your hands, then here are some options:

1. Suffer stoically, buy a rinse to hide the grey hairs and wait for age and maturity to bring about better behaviour.

2. Use grandma, a neighbour or occasional care to allow tantrum free shopping.

3. Use late night shopping or bring your partner on a Saturday as an extra pair of arms, a minder and entertainer.

4. Choose supermarkets that have a chocolate-free checkout and use it.

5. Set up a distraction before you get to the section of the supermarket where you know the problem lies. 'Look, there's a man with funny-looking hair!' is always a good ploy.

6. When all else fails, opt for smash and grab shopping. The S and G shopper knows exactly what she wants to buy before leaving home. She enters the supermarket, toddler in tow, with sparks flying from the trolley wheels. She speeds round, scooping products from the shelves, with direction, determination and not a hint of hesitation, then through the checkout, pay and away. If you are lucky, this leaves the stunned little spectator still revving up for his usual supermarket performance, but it is all too late.

Most children who throw a tantrum when outside do the same at home. It is sensible to focus first on the tantrums at home and once these have been tidied up, this control usually spreads to outside.

# EIGHT

# Toilet Training

Children become toilet trained when they, and only they, are ready. No child can be trained until the appropriate nerve pathways have sufficiently matured, a process that is completely outside the influence of even the most brilliant parent or doctor.

Once sufficiently mature, the process is controlled by the child's will to comply or his determination to defy. In turn, this is dependent on the child's temperament, as well as the skill and cunning of the trainer.

Most toilet training difficulties today are really non-problems caused by unrealistic expectations and misleading advice. Turn a deaf ear to all those well-meaning but interfering friends and family. Do not start too early: this invariably leads to unnecessary problems. Remember that the child alone has the ultimate power to go where and when he wishes. Don't hurry, don't fight, just relax.

## Toileting: normal development

During the first $1\frac{1}{2}$ years of life there is no proper bowel or bladder control, just the toilet timing reflex. As the child approaches 18 months this reflex appears to weaken and voluntary control begins to take over.

It is pointless to consider serious toilet training until

the child knows at least when he is wet or dirty. In the months that follow this discovery, the child becomes aware of his toileting needs before the event rather than after. This great breakthrough occurs somewhere between **18 months and 2 years of age**, but with urine training there is one unfortunate flaw. Although warning is given, the child's alarm system is only adjusted to tell of the impending puddle five seconds before it arrives.

**By the age of 2**, the amount of warning has increased and you can start to notch up a few successes. At about this time bowel control will also become established, in some children before urine control and in others after it.

**By the age of 2½ years**, over two-thirds of children will be dry most of the time; the majority can take themselves to the toilet and handle their pants without too many mistakes. At this age night-time wetting also starts to come under control, the child initially needing to be lifted onto the toilet in the middle of the night, and later holding on unaided. Although most children are dry

> You can't go too far wrong with toilet training as long as you don't start too early, don't force the child, and just take your time.

and bowel trained by the age of $2\frac{1}{2}$, the whole procedure is still surrounded by a great sense of urgency – the child needing to go 'now' rather than when it suits the parents.

Early toilet training is no more a sign of intelligence than early development of teeth. Our teaching today is clear:

- Eighteen months is the earliest age to consider toilet training.

- Two years is probably a more realistic time and if you wait till $2\frac{1}{2}$, it won't worry me.

- Forcing little children causes tension and tension causes little humans to clamp closed all bodily openings. Don't force – relax. Relaxed little children find toileting easiest.

A decision that parents have to make is whether to train toddlers to use the toilet or a potty. There is no right answer to this; the method of using them is more important than the equipment itself.

Most parents start their child sitting on the potty, and most toddlers prefer this to the toilet. It has the great advantage of being portable, so it can be taken from room to room. There are, however, a number of independent little toddlers who wish to use the toilet like grown ups. If this is the case, a small child's toilet seat should be put inside the adult one.

# The fundamental rules

1. A child must first learn to sit on the toilet before he can learn to open his bowels on that toilet.

2. A child must know the difference between feeling wet and dry before he can be bladder trained.

3. A child must be able to produce some dry nappies at night before you can expect a dry bed.

## Bladder training – the plan

- Are they old enough to start training?

- Do they know the difference between wet and dry?

- If your carpets can cope, use pants.

- Sit the child regularly before mealtimes and as a double act when toileting yourself.

- Don't force, don't stir, drop subtle hints of encouragement.

- When it eventually happens, notice and reward.

## Boys: should they sit or stand?

Some experts philosophise painfully over the pros and cons of whether little boys should learn to wee standing or sitting. It honestly doesn't matter one little bit. If you opt for standing, urine training may come fractionally faster due to the rewards of hearing so much tinkling water and also being in charge of one's own equipment.

There are, however, several drawbacks. Toddlers at this age are prone to what I call the 'Fireman Syndrome' – they are hellishly inaccurate and spray water all over the place.

In addition, some get so carried away with this new skill that it's almost impossible to ever get them to sit. So you've promoted urine training but delayed the bowel habit. If your child gets locked into standing and resists sitting, don't worry, this is only a temporary problem.

### Bowel training – the plan

- Start after 18 months of age at a time when both parents and child are ready.

- Sit the child three times a day after meals. Make it fun. Never force. Don't make a fuss over defiance.

- Once sitting is established give a gentle emotional nudge of encouragement which plants the seeds of success and then wait patiently.

- When the big day arrives – set off the fireworks!

## Toddler urgency

When you are out shopping with a toddler, you learn very quickly that when he says 'Wee wee, now,' he means now – and not in five minutes. At this age, parents are forced to throw modesty to the wind, aiming the child towards the gutter or helping him water the nearby flowerbed. Car travel is also difficult, with frequent stops often being required. Urgency is normal in toddlers. Small patches of dampness appear, particularly when the child is excited or engrossed in play. Major accidents also happen for at least a year.

## Toddler bed wetting

The average age of attaining night-time dryness is about 33 months, but 10 per cent of 5-year-olds still wet their bed regularly. After this age, about 15 per cent of them are cured of the habit each year, until it becomes relatively rare in the teenager. The parents of the 5-year-old who wets his bed must be reassured that, although other parents are not openly declaring the fact, two other children in their child's class will also be regular bed wetters.

Delay in bladder training at night seems to have an extremely strong genetic relationship. Some studies show almost 70 per cent of wetters have a parent or sibling with a similar problem. Bed wetting is also more common in boys.

## Treatment for bed wetting

- When you find a number of night nappies make it through to morning still dry, it is time to take them off. For most this accelerates the training.

- If bladder control remains unreliable, lift and take the child to the toilet before you go to bed. This suits some and helps them stay dry.

- Medication is known to help some but the effect is temporary.

- When 6 years and still wet, get a bedwetting alarm. The results are excellent.

# NINE

# Sleep

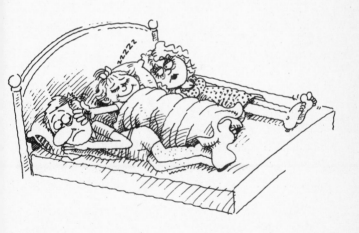

Toddlers who don't sleep well can be the cause of great unhappiness to their parents. The mother who says, 'He's not getting enough sleep,' is in fact talking in code. What she really means is, 'Forget the kid, I'm a walking zombie'.

The night-time antics are really only half the story. It is the after-shock the next day that causes the real harm. Then a tired, irritable mum with a befuddled brain has to struggle valiantly to manage a tired, irritable and unreasonable toddler. The result is often complete disaster.

If you are an exhausted reader, with a sleepless toddler, relief is now in sight. The methods that follow offer a 90 per cent chance of cure within a week.

## Sleep problems – the main offenders

When it comes to sleep, there are three strategies children use to pain their parents. The most damaging is that *middle-of-the-night wakening*, where the child cries once or many times night after night and month after month. This can turn happy smiling people into the 'living dead'. Then there are those who *won't settle when put down at night*. This does not exhaust parents or deprive them of sleep but it robs them of valuable time alone together. Lastly, there is the child who goes down alright but then in the wee small hours *wriggles his way silently into his parents' bed*. By itself this is a fairly innocent habit but as many night visitors also kick and push parents out the side, this is not much fun.

Children wake on other occasions when they are sick, teething, frightened or when home life is disrupted and of course these are not sleep problems. At times like this children need comfort, not discipline.

## The controlled crying technique

All adults and most children learn to wake, roll over and put themselves back to sleep without disturbing the household. When toddlers are comforted, fed and fussed over every time they come near the surface, the chances are that they will wake regularly to capitalise on so much good attention. When comfort is not readily available to toddlers, they generally decide it is easier to settle themselves and go back to sleep.

Controlled crying refers to my method of letting children cry for a short period, then coming in to give some, but not full comfort, letting them cry a little longer each time, giving more incomplete comfort, gradually increasing the crying time between comforting.

# The science of sleep

Sleep is not one consistent state of unconsciousness, it is a cycle of deep, light and dream sleep punctuated with regular brief periods of waking. Brain-wave studies (EEGs) back this up. These show a different electrical pattern for each stage. First we drift off to sleep, then hit the deepest plane of unconsciousness, we dream for a while, then lift to a lighter state before coming briefly to consciousness, to stretch, turn over then drift off again for a re-run of the cycle.

These electrical tracings indicate that the average newborn has a sleep cycle of just under 1 hour, a toddler about 1¼ hours, whilst we adults go about 1½ hours between awakenings.

We have to accept that all humans will wake regularly each night, but we do not have to accept that human children should disturb their parents when they do wake. It is normal for children to wake briefly throughout the night. They can kick, wake, grumble and make some noise but they cannot expect you to share in their nocturnal activities. Toddlers should be encouraged to act like adults and learn to settle themselves back to sleep.

Eventually they think: 'I know she loves me, I know she will always come but it is just not worth all the effort'.

## The technique

■ Toddler wakes at 3 a.m. Initially there is gentle crying, which soon turns to a noisy protest.

■ Leave them crying for 5 minutes if you are average, 10 minutes if you are tough, 2 minutes if you are delicate and 1 minute if you are very fragile. The length of crying depends on the tolerance of parents and how genuinely upset the child becomes. Don't give in easily to grumbling or noisy crying with dry tears, but genuine upset with fear and hysteria needs quick comfort.

■ Go into the toddler's room; lift, cuddle, comfort. Occasionally you can get away with patting them as they lie in the cot, which is all the better.

■ When loud, upset crying turns to sobs and sniffs, this is the God-given signal to put them down and walk out decisively.

■ They are taken aback that you dared to walk out. Immediately they start crying again in protest.

■ Now leave them to cry 2 minutes longer than the previous period (10 + 2 minutes, 5 + 2 minutes, 2 + 2 minutes, 1 + 2 minutes).

■ Go in, lift, cuddle, talk, comfort. At the moment the crying comes towards control, put them down and exit immediately.

■ Once again increase the period of crying by 2 minutes. Then comfort, increase period of the crying again, comfort, increase, etc.

■ Be extremely firm, continue for as long as it takes. It is pointless starting this technique unless you are prepared to see it through.

■ Once they fall asleep, get yourself back to bed and try to get some rest. If they wake again, once more be completely firm. Do the same tomorrow night, the night after and for as long as it is needed.

■ If no success is in sight and you are approaching the limit of your endurance, don't give up, combine the technique with a small dose of sedation for several nights.

■ After half an hour of unsuccessful controlled crying technique, give sedation. This will take a further half hour to act and in this period, keep the technique going with firm resolve. With sedation you are guaranteed to get your sleep after an hour and the child still hears a very firm and consistent message before finally dropping off. Sedation is strictly short term.

■ It can be helpful to get a friend to act as a 'sponsor'. As you struggle away at 2 a.m. trying to be tough, it is a whole lot easier to be firm if you have to report your efforts to someone outside the combat area in the morning.

## When they won't go to bed at night

Over half of all toddlers will play up when it is time for bed if they know they can get away with it. They seem to be designed with a sleep clock whose bedtime is considerably later than the setting their parents would wish. Some are tired but still obstinately refuse to go to bed, while others infuriate their parents by popping in and out of their rooms like a Jack-in-the-Box. Other, more subtle toddlers, create a smokescreen of requests for drinks, the toilet and various comforters, which succeed in keeping parents on the hop and gain them great attention. Most bedtime problems are simply bad habits which can be avoided with routine and rules administered by gentle but determined parents. Here are some suggestions.

## The gentle approach

*Good routine* Try to follow a regular routine in the lead-up to bed, then put them down at a constant bedtime. Where settling poses a problem, a later bedtime may be introduced on a temporary basis. Once this is well established it is quite easy to bring it forward a few minutes each night, until an acceptable level is achieved.

*Calm them down* Don't fight, stir, run, chase or play wild games near bedtime. Olympic athletes do not finish the race and then go straight to sleep and we ourselves need to unwind before bed. Bath, talk, tuck up, cuddle and read a soothing story.

*Leave decisively* When it is time to go, say goodnight and leave as though you mean it. Do not rise to requests whose only purpose is procrastination.

*If they come out* If they reappear you must be firm. Don't feel guilty at being tough, after all you have given them your absolute best attention before bedtime. Never encourage Jack-in-the-Box behaviour. You put them back once, no questions are accepted, you know you are in charge, they know where they stand and that is it.

## The tough option

*Good routine, calm down, leave decisively* As above.

*If they come out once* Put them back immediately. Leave them in no doubt that you are not going to tolerate this and will be extremely heavy if they reappear.

*If they come out again* At this point there must be no misunderstandings. You dearly love them but you have given them a more than generous amount of your time and attention and if as much as a nose pokes out again, you will descend like lightning from Mount Olympus.

*If they come out yet again* At this point a serious challenge is being staged and you can either stand up and be decisive or decide to abdicate your position as a credible leader. If you mean business, you must block all routes of escape. If you believe in giving a warning smack, this is the time to consider it.

## Green's patent rope trick

If parents realise that they are rapidly getting nowhere, I strongly recommend the rope trick. This is one of my better inventions, which came from the drawing board when I was trying to curb the escape-artist antics of my own children. All that is required is a short length of strong rope.

Before you get worried, I am not going to suggest that you tie your child to the bed, tempting though this might on occasion be. What you do is loop one end of the rope around the inner handle of the bedroom door and attach the other end to the handle of a nearby door.

Carefully adjust the rope so that when the bedroom door is forced open, the aperture is just a little less than the diameter of the offending child's head. As all of you who have had babies know, if the head is not going to get out, nothing is. It is not that they are locked in, they just cannot get out.

With your child safely in his room, he may resort to crying to break your resolve but once again this ploy will fail as you use the controlled crying technique. A light should be left on in the passageway outside the bedroom, so that the child can see and hear what is going on around the house. This means that the child will not become frightened, yet at the same time he is made very aware that bed is the place he is meant to be.

This is not a way of making children go to sleep, it is only a means of ensuring that when you put them to bed they stay there!

## The child who comes to his parents' bed each night

Coming to the parents' bed in the middle of the night constitutes the least damaging of the three major sleep problems of toddlerhood. It is up to the individual parent to decide whether to tolerate this behaviour or have a showdown.

The methods outlined below may seem rather harsh but the middle of the night is no time for playing games, and it is worth being firm, because the chances of a quick and permanent cure are excellent.

## The technique

- The moment the child appears he must be put back immediately.

- If the child returns, give a stern warning and, if possible, have the other parent return him to bed.

- If he returns a third time, immobilise doors.

- The results: ten out of ten cured if that is what you really want.

## Common questions

*'I have tried your controlled crying technique and it does not work.'*

When I get the exact details of what has been done, the questioner has usually missed the point of my method. Make sure you have used the technique correctly. You must be committed to a cure and be totally firm, especially in the middle of the night. When you appear to be getting nowhere, short-term sedation in association with the technique is necessary. This allows parents to remain rested and resolute even through a quite prolonged campaign. When performed properly, it is extremely rare that a cure, or at least a significant improvement, cannot be achieved.

*'He shares a room with his sister and if we try your crying technique they both will be awake all night.'*
It is surprising how many siblings are able to sleep through all this crying. When the disturbance is genuine and not being raised by the parents as a red herring, I suggest that the other child is moved to a different bedroom and if this is not available, to the furthest corner of the house. Having isolated the offending party, you are now able to perform my technique properly and within a week, two sleep-loving children will be together again.

*'He cries at night and if I go in immediately and insert a dummy there is instant peace. Should I use your technique?'*
If we were being completely sensible about discipline, the dummy would be removed, the controlled crying technique used and the problem would be finished within a few days. Having said this, it is often easier for most of us to insert the dummy, knowing that minor disturbances like this are remarkably short lived. We don't need to bring our children up exactly by the book.

If the parents and child are reasonably rested, happy and peaceful then that is good enough, without worrying about minor infringements.

*'I have used your technique effectively in the middle of the night, but what do I do when he wakes at 5.30 a.m.?'*
This is a common question which is hard to answer. If you are tough at this hour and use the controlled crying technique, by the time he falls asleep you are ready to get up for the day and it all seems a bit pointless. Sedation so late also leaves hangovers during the day. Occasionally changing to a later bedtime or cutting out the afternoon sleep will work. Often it is better to accept an early start to the day and get up with the toddler.

Sleep problems can affect the whole family – and sometimes the whole neighbourhood. Ask yourself *'Is this sleep problem worth the effort of changing?'* Remember many problems will settle with time.

# TEN

# Eating

Food is the fuel that powers our young children. It makes them grow strong, gives them pleasure and provides them with many opportunities to wind up their parents. We can choose the healthiest designer diet, put it on a plate, even get it into the mouth, but if they decide that's as far as it is going: checkmate – the game is over!

As parents, let's aim to loosen up a bit, stick to realistic expectations of diet and never let food become a battle. We should also set a good example, and where better to begin than at the start of toddlerhood. There we have complete control over the available diet. After all, we are the ones who buy the stuff.

## What is a balanced diet?

Adults and toddlers need six different types of nourishment to survive: protein, carbohydrate, fats, vitamins, minerals and water.

*Protein* is present in meat, eggs and cheese; lesser quality vegetable proteins are found in beans, nuts, etc.

*Carbohydrate* comes in simple forms as glucose, sucrose (cane sugar) or more complex form as the starches in cereals, bread, pasta, vegetables, fruit, nuts and so on. The simple sugars are easy to eat, and often come partnered with fat, making an irresistible taste combination, so it is easy to eat too much. Complex carbohydrates have much more bulk than the simple sugars, which means it is not so easy to overindulge and thus become overweight. Complex carbohydrate, once the in-food for athletes, is now reckoned to be the in-food for all of us.

*Fats* are present in meat, cooking oils, milk, butter, cheese, nuts, etc. There are two types of fat, the saturated sort mostly found in animal products and the unsaturated type more often derived from vegetable sources. Fats are an important source of energy, providing double that of the same amount of sugar and putting on twice the amount of weight if we are not careful. Though reduced fat diets are important for adults and older children, young toddlers burn up so much energy with their activity and growth that a reasonable amount of fat does not seem a problem.

*Vitamins* are required in small quantities if we are to remain healthy. Once we have the desired amount, doubling or trebling these levels does not make us twice or three times as fit; in fact it does nothing. There are various vitamins such as vitamin C which is found in fruits and juices, and vitamin D which is present in eggs and butter as well as being manufactured by sunshine acting on our skin. There is a great deal of misleading advertising about vitamins. Australian children who do not have some major bowel or other medical condition will be getting all the vitamins needed if they are given a half reasonable toddler diet.

*Minerals* are required in small amounts. Iron and calcium are the two we think of most. Iron is found in large quantities in meat and lesser quantities in fortified cereals, bread and some vegetables. Toddlers who do not eat these can become short of iron. Calcium comes mainly from dairy foods and it may be low in a child who takes absolutely none of these in any of their varied forms.

*Water* is required in large amounts and what better way to take it than straight from the tap. In this form it has even fewer calories than Diet Coke and your dentist, no matter what his religion, will bless it. Most of our water is now fluoridated and despite various ill-informed pronouncements, this is safe. As for other pollutants, we

# He won't eat his vegetables

Modern nutritional science has proved something that we all know anyway: vegetables are very important foods. They contain not only fibre, complex carbohydrates and vitamins, but also many protective factors that prevent chronic diseases in adulthood. Unfortunately vegetables turn out to be children's least favourite food. And, let's face it, many adults do not find them particularly mouth-watering.

When it comes to vegetables and toddlers, the story is quite simple. Try to introduce small amounts, different tastes and lots of variety from the earliest days. If your little ones enjoy them that is great, if not don't force the issue.

Experiment with the full spectrum of vegies, from greens to beans and back again. If all this is a non-event, don't worry, fruit (and fruit juice) can substitute for vegetables. But remember, keep offering small amounts of vegetables without any force. Research has shown that persistence without pressure is the key to success.

can protest about discolouration or too much chlorine, but the water we use must be purer and safer than that available to 90 per cent of the world's population.

# Feed – don't fight

Parents use up an enormous amount of energy forcing stubborn but otherwise well-nourished toddlers to eat against their will. Playing aeroplanes and dive bombers are a complete waste of time. What they really need is gentle encouragement. Toddlers have minds and tastes of their own – the dining table must never become a battle-ground.

## The ten-point plan for problem-free meals

1. Avoid disorganised, disturbed, noisy mealtimes. The toddler should sit and eat with the rest of the family, but if this is impractical then a parent should sit next to the child and feed him before the main family meal.

2. Although the toddler should ideally be given a variety of well-balanced foods, if he dislikes variety, then a repetitive but nutritious diet is perfectly acceptable. After all he's the one who has to eat it, not you.

3. Adult eating habits should be encouraged, but it is no disaster if a child decides to return to the main course after having polished off his pudding.

4. Use labour-saving cooking ideas, because it is hard to stay calm when the wilful toddler refuses a dish that has taken hours to prepare.

5. Gently encourage the child to eat, NEVER force.

6. Once it is obvious that the child is not going to eat any more, wipe his hands and face clean and allow him to get down from the table. Whether this is after five minutes or half an hour, don't worry about it. If the child is dawdling over his food, leave him to dawdle without an audience.

7. Display no anger if food is not eaten. Put the untouched plate in the fridge and bring it out later on request.

8. It is the child's right to eat or not to eat his food as he pleases. Parents have a perfect right to fight with their child if that is what they want, but they should have the sense to avoid battles over food. If a child refuses the meal, he must not be allowed to immediately top up on milk, chips and the like.

9. Don't fuss if children prefer picking foods up with hands rather than using spoons or other eating utensils. Hands are fine and minimise washing up.

10. Never let children run around eating. Make sure they sit down. Choking on food is a real problem.

## Choking on food

Young children do not have the back teeth needed to chew and grind lumps of food properly; these may not be fully developed until around 4 years of age. Young children are still learning to eat solid food.

Food swallowed in large pieces is more likely to get stuck and block off the airways. If it goes 'down the wrong way' this can cause young children to choke.

If young children run, play, laugh or cry while eating they are more likely to choke on their food.

### How to make eating safer for young children

*Food:*

■ Do not give food that can break off into hard pieces.

■ Avoid raw carrot, celery sticks and apple pieces, for example. These foods should be grated, cooked or mashed.

■ Sausages, frankfurts and other meats should be cut into small pieces. Tough skins on frankfurts and other sausages should be removed.

■ Do not give popcorn, nuts, hard lollies, cornchips or other similar foods to young children.

*At eating times:*
■ Always stay with young children and supervise them while eating.

■ Make sure that young children sit quietly while eating.

■ Never force young children to eat, as this may cause them to choke.

## What to do if a young child chokes on food

*If the child is breathing, coughing or crying, the child may be able to dislodge the food by coughing:*

■ Do not try to dislodge the food by hitting the child on the back because this may move the food into a more dangerous position and make the child stop breathing.

■ Stay with the child and watch to see if their breathing improves.

■ If the child is not breathing easily within a few minutes, phone 999 for an ambulance.

*If the child is not breathing:*

- Try to dislodge the piece of food by placing the child face down over your lap so that their head is lower than their chest.

- Give the child four sharp blows on the back just between the shoulder blades. This should provide enough force to dislodge the food.

- Check again for signs of breathing.

- **If the child is still not breathing, urgently call 999 and ask for an ambulance. The ambulance service operator will be able to tell you what to do next.**

(Courtesy, Women's and Children's Hospital, Adelaide.)

# Make food fun

When serving fine food to adults, a chef prides himself not only on the taste but also on the presentation. The same should apply when feeding toddlers.

For a start, portions should not be massive. Various garnishes should be used, such as a square of cheese, some raisins and a few fingers of fruit. Vary texture and colour wherever possible and make food look appealing. Bread can be cut into fun triangles and homemade biscuits can be baked in animal shapes.

When feeding problems continue, then try varying the venue. Wonders can be achieved by transporting stubborn feeders to the balcony or the garden, where they can drink milk through a straw and eat little sandwiches out of a lunch box.

I think we have to rid ourselves of some of our rigid and old-fashioned ideas about feeding toddlers. Within reason, try to give them what they want, where they want it, and when they are hungry. They are going to have to learn adult eating habits sooner or later, but to begin with it is more important to get them enjoying the process of eating.

## The toddler who's hooked on bottles and baby food

For the younger toddler who is hooked on milk and refuses solids, it is hard to give effective help without cutting down dramatically on the milk intake. The milk intake should be reduced by about half and other fluids and a variety of interesting nibbly things introduced. This is usually all that is required, but if it does not work immediately then the milk can be further reduced. Like all such procedures, the parent must not weaken mid-way.

Firmness is also needed with toddlers who have remained on slushy baby foods for too long. These children often refuse to chew and the slightest lump causes them to gag. Somehow, however, they seem to exert some hidden strength when a piece of chocolate is popped into their mouths.

Once again, prevention is better than cure, as these children will often put up quite a fight before you can get them onto a normal diet. To cure these children, start again by halving the milk intake so that it cannot be used as a substitute food. Then gradually start polluting tinned baby food with homemade semi-liquidised products and, as the days go by, make the food more and more homemade. Gradually a normal diet is achieved in a matter of weeks.

## What is enough food intake?

Children have different food requirements. They eat like birds: some like sparrows, others like vultures. There is no correct amount of food for all children to consume in a day. Food intake and growth are not the only indicators of good health, energy is also important. If my car used only half the manufacturer's recommended amount of petrol to cover a given number of kilometres, I would not complain. I would

**If our children are growing well and are healthy, there cannot be too much wrong with their food intake.**

be grateful that I had an efficient machine that was obviously tuned to perfection. Most toddlers whose parents claim that they never eat are in fact getting a very adequate food intake.

If children wish to eat three good meals a day, that is highly commendable, but for those who don't, it is usually better to provide nourishing snacks rather than fighting with them. Time and peer-group pressures will eventually force the toddler into more traditional meal-time habits; in the meantime, be flexible and use your imagination.

Remember, food is not just for nourishment, food is for fun.

## Consider the toddler's point of view

It is a very special occasion and you are booked to eat at the best restaurant in town. Out comes the food, immaculate with those cordon bleu sauces flowing off the meat. Your mouth is watering at the very smell.

Then up marches the head waiter, who looks you in the eye and with a stern voice says: 'Just one thing, madam. You will not be leaving the table until you've eaten every bite. What's more there will be no dessert until your plate is completely clear.' Would it not make you choke?

A minute later there beside you is the chef. He takes out a large carving knife and fork and proceeds to cut up your meat into little pieces, mashes it all up with the vegetables and starts spooning it into your mouth.

Just put yourself in your child's place. Why should he like it any more than you would? Get off their backs and don't fight over food.

# ELEVEN

# Nasty Habits

In those dreamy days before toddlers, I bet you never saw yourself reading and recognising your children in a chapter like this. Now you may well have found that the nicest of nice children can display some of the nastiest of nasty habits. Let's look at a selection of these.

## Biting

In my experience, biting is a playground habit found mostly in the 1 to 2½ years age group. It is not a pre-meditated, spiteful act, just a symptom of this age of little sense. It is usually a piece of brother or sister that finds itself wedged between the closing teeth and as this is a sort of family feast, it is much easier to discipline, as you own both the biter and the bitee.

When it is a neighbour's child that has been nibbled, the parents may expect you to instigate some sort of major retribution. If justice is not seen to be done, friends may ban their little children from your house and it can lead to family feuds more vicious than that of the Montagues and Capulets.

**Even the nicest children can develop some nasty habits.**

How you react to a bite will depend on the circumstances. If just a minor nip in times of excitement, a gentle warning is all that is needed. If it is repeated in a major way and a stern warning has been ignored, then use Time Out. If this has failed, some parents will give a short sharp smack to register the limits of acceptable behaviour.

When your toddler bites another at playgroup, this is a different matter. Now you are in the full public view, without Time Out to fall back on and if you smack, half the audience will criticise. It is particularly embarrassing when your loved one has become known as 'Jaws' to the other mums. The best you can do is to watch carefully, warn firmly, divert when an impending attack is antici- pated and then, if a bite occurs, ignore the biter and give the best toys and attention to the injured party. This may sound rather wishy-washy but when outside the home, your hands are tied and in truth your child prob- ably has more teeth than any technique I may suggest.

Don't despair – remember that biting is only a habit of the first 2½ years and be reassured that they will not be going round biting others as adults.

## Finger up the nose

Little noses are to little fingers like a burrow is to a bunny. It is a comfortable place to explore when there is nothing better to do. The toddler watches the TV, is

# Won't buckle up

Experts tell us that when we are going out in the car we should put the child into his car seat and we should not drive off unless the seat belt is done up. But there are some children who refuse to stay in their seat.

If your child won't stay in his seat, pull over to the side of the road and don't move off until you have him back in the seat and buckled up. Look your child in the eye and speak firmly: 'This car will not move unless you have your belt done up'. If it happens again, give another warning. After several warnings you have run out of options.

A child roaming around in the car is very dangerous. If there is an accident the child may be killed. If the police pull you over you will be fined heavily. The police won't be impressed when you tell them 'I can't make my 2-year-old stay in his seat'.

I don't like smacking children but now is the time you may choose to use one. Give a clear warning, 'If you undo your belt one more time I will smack you'. Be firm, don't feel guilty, and carry it through.

bored, his mind slips and with it a finger, ever upward and inward. You can only sympathise with the problem, such is the standard of today's television.

Though most toddler fingers find toddler nostrils at times of tiredness or boredom, occasionally an older child with an easily baited parent will do it just to annoy. When this happens, it is best to ignore, divert to something more useful and if you decide to take notice, don't make a game out of it, be 100 per cent firm.

With toddlers, the aim is to divert them and keep those little hands and minds fully occupied.

## Head banging

Head banging is a habit which can occur for one of two reasons. Usually it is part of a tantrum in the senseless 1 to 2-year-old, though it may be a form of innocent entertainment in the child of a slightly older age.

Head banging tantrums are short lived, as the child soon develops sufficient sense to realise that self-inflicted pain is a poor way of punishing others. Head banging is quite self-limiting and all you have to do is divert attention elsewhere. If that's difficult, just let them go for it. Toddlers may have little sense but they are not stupid. Whatever you do, this habit will be well away by the age of 2 years.

Some children head bang when bored or tired. This is usually the speciality of active children who enjoy rocking and gentle head banging, particularly in the cot. They do it because it is enjoyable and sends them to sleep as reliably as counting sheep. Though it may be soothing for children, the rhythmic thump is far from soothing for the adults of the house. There is not much you can do about it other than padding the edge of the cot, or in extreme cases, putting a pillow under each cot leg to deaden the transmission of sound. This sort of head banging is not a sign of bad behaviour but a form of innocent entertainment that gives as much pleasure as thumb sucking.

## Playing with their private parts

Most toddlers play with their genitalia at some time or other. They may touch, rub, rock or move their legs, all for the pleasurable effects these motions afford. It is normal toddler behaviour, and it has no true sexual overtones.

Historically, so much fuss has been made over children masturbating that even the most broad-minded parents still have a twinge of concern when they see their children doing it.

These days, parents are encouraged to relax, ignore it and not let their own hang-ups get in the way. Playing with the genitalia occurs in both boys

**Most nasty habits are innocent and pass with maturity**

and girls. It starts in the second year when the nappy region is unveiled and a new area of discovery is made available. The treatment is to completely ignore what is, after all, a perfectly innocent habit.

Now it is all very easy for me to say ignore but what do you do when the child is standing in church with his hands down his pants, or when friends are visiting? In fact it is probably more realistic to gently divert the offending hand or interest the child in something more sociable. I emphasise that at toddler age this has no sexual connotations and it almost exclusively happens when they are tired, tense or bored. Ignoring, diversion and keeping them active is the answer – not humilia- tion or punishment.

## Whingeing

Whingeing is one of the most parent-destroying activi- ties that any child can indulge in. Naturally we expect children who are tired, sick or teething to whinge but there still remains a great band of healthy, well-rested children who continue to devastate their parents.

There is a great variation in a child's ability to whinge. Some never whinge at all, others wind up to full volume at the drop of a hat, whilst some work their way up in fits and starts, prolonging the agony as skilfully as any torture in the Spanish Inquisition.

The trouble with whingeing is that we can unintentionally make it into a much repeated behaviour by the way we act. The 4-year-old is not allowed out to play because it is raining. He complains and whinges. This gets particularly painful after ten minutes so you repent in order to preserve your sanity. Now you have blown it. You have set a precedent that a definite 'No' can be turned to an equally definite 'Yes' if you whinge long enough. This is not a wise way to run things:

■ Skilful mothers can divert lesser whingers back to the straight and narrow by noticing something around the house or setting off on some interesting activity. This strategy can be of some benefit in the not-very-determined whinger.

■ If diversion does not work, the child must be ignored. Mortal man has only a limited ability to actually ignore whingeing, so pretending to ignore it is probably the best we can hope for. It still gives an equally strong message to the offending party.

- When the parents can no longer ignore the irritation, and the situation is coming close to a blow-up when somebody is going to lose control, this is the moment to employ the Time Out technique. This avoids a loss of control when everyone would become very unhappy, and little would be achieved.

- As a last resort, when diversion, ignoring and Time Out have all failed, mother must sweep up the offending party and head for the great outdoors. Most children suspend hostilities as soon as they escape from the restrictions of the home battleground, and with the minority who continue, the whingeing never seems so bad when competing with bird song and noisy motor vehicles.

## The absconder

Any toddler worth his salt, and who has read up on his child psychology, will realise that he is meant to be clingy and loath to be separated from his parents. A small percentage, however, seem ignorant of this fact, and they are forever running off and getting lost. Absconders are a real trial to their parents, who are forced to take part in high speed pursuits down the main street, hide and seek in the supermarket and the interminable wait for the voice to come over the loud-speaker informing them that the infant absconder has been corralled and is awaiting pick-up. If your child is an absconder, make sure he is wearing a luggage label like Paddington Bear.

Luckily most absconders develop sufficient sense to stop the habit within a six-month period but some may take years to grow out of it. I am able only to suggest that the parents remain fit and vigilant at all times, or resort to toddler reins.

So there you have it, even the nicest children can develop some nasty habits. Most of these problems are innocent and pass with maturity. While waiting for this to happen, focus on the light at the end of the tunnel and steer calmly in that direction.

# TWELVE

# Fears, Comforters and Family Tension

However foolish a child's fears may seem to an adult, they are very real to the child, and they must not be put down or ridiculed. The best way to treat childhood fears is by good parental example, lots of support and comfort, and then gradual desensitisation. There is usually no reason to get too worried, as most fears at this age are temporary problems that evaporate with the passage of time.

## Different fears for different years

It's normal for children to have different fears at different years. At birth, babies are relatively immune to fears. The only things that startle the newborn are sudden movement and noise.

**From birth to 6 months** there is little change, then somewhere around the seventh month the baby suddenly becomes inseparable from his main caretaker, usually his mother.

**At 1 year** this separation is still a major problem. The child may also dislike loud noises, such as doorbells, vacuum cleaners or food mixers. Strange people, strange objects and sudden movements can also cause him distress.

**At the age of 2** the fear of separation still exists but it becomes slightly less intense and more predictable than in the 1-year-old. Loud noises still cause upsets, as will the unexpected ambulance sirens or the violent barking of dogs.

**Between 2 and 4 years** a whole new package of fears starts to emerge; animals and the dark featuring prominently. The fear of animals hits its peak around the age of 3; fear of the dark usually peaks nearer the fifth birthday.

All young children have one overwhelming fear in common – the fear of being separated from their parents.

## Separation

The fear of separation is common to all toddlers from the age of about 7 months, until it wanes by pre-school age. It is at its most intense in the early years, its ebb varying greatly from child to child and family to family.

Initially, the child resents being handled by anyone except his mother, but this quickly eases to allow all the other members of the family and close friends in on the act. When playing, he is never far from mum, and if outside or playing in another room, he reappears every few minutes to reassure himself of her presence.

Most parents need babysitters at one time or another. The ideal babysitter is a grandparent, other relative or close friend. Leaving the child with other babysitters may be difficult initially, with profuse tears being shed on departure and again at pick-up time. Between these times there is usually relative happiness which can be confirmed by one quick phone call. The child should be accompanied by his cuddly toys and security items, and he should never be left in a great rush.

# Comforters and security blankets

Children are not the only ones to enjoy comforters. Adults enjoy them too. Toddler comforters generally consist of thumbs, dummies, teddy bears and security blankets. There's nothing intrinsically wrong with any of these, as long as the habit does not last too long.

## Thumb sucking

Children seem to suck their thumbs when they are tired, bored, frustrated or tense. It is also a good way of getting to sleep. In times of stress, and particularly when a new baby arrives, many toddlers regress to this old habit. By the age of $3^{1}/_{2}$, most children have spontaneously removed their thumbs from their mouths, although some studies suggest that up to 2 per cent still have this habit in their early teens.

The only worry with thumb sucking is that it can cause teeth to become displaced and stick out. Certainly before the age of 6, thumb sucking does not damage permanent teeth. After that, it takes more than just a few minutes of thumb in mouth at bedtime to cause harm.

Below the age of 4 years I believe that thumb sucking should be totally ignored. After this, hands can be subtly diverted and bodies can be busied onto something more productive. Rewards for 'grown up behaviour' can be given, but whatever happens it must never become the cause of a fight or the child will continue it, just to annoy.

## Dummies, pacifiers and comforters

Most doctors have an inbuilt dislike of these, but no-one has ever found any evidence to indicate that they do any harm. Objection to them is more on aesthetic grounds than medical ones. It is claimed that they are unhygienic, but so are the ten dirty fingers that would be inserted in the mouth if the dummy was not there. Many parents are determined never to resort to these pacifiers but relent when confronted with an extremely irritable, difficult child. If the dummy helps in those situations, then good luck to them.

Although I do not like dummies, I assure parents that they do not cause any harm. When the time is right, preferably before 2½, discard the object nevertheless. It has to go some time. It is usually best to be brave, throw it away, and then brace yourself for the repercussions. Those who do not have the courage to discard it so abruptly may try a gradual withdrawal by losing it or accidentally damaging it. After 3½ the child may well be reasoned with and the dummy given up after some hard bargaining.

## Teddies, cuddlies and security blankets

Most youngsters have some object that they seek out and cuddle up to when tired or upset. This can be some exotic imported stuffed animal, mum's own battered but much-loved teddy, a sheepskin rug or even a rapidly disintegrating bit of old fabric. Whatever the 'real-world' value of the object, in the eyes of the child it is priceless. These items are often referred to as 'transition objects'. They give security, continuity and comfort to a child when the environment and those in it are changing. It is his link with his home base when he starts day care.

Comforters and transition objects are normal, natural and healthy. They promote, rather than postpone, security. Like Christopher Robin and his trusty bear, Pooh, the young child armed with his blanket can accomplish many a daring feat that would never have been possible alone.

## Tags and touchers

Parents can spend big bucks on a top-of-the-line toy, but all that interests their infant is the maker's tag. Some twist this round a finger as they settle to sleep, while others love to rub the silky label against their skin. The ultimate comfort experience is to clutch a teddy, suck a bottle and twiddle a tag, all in unison. Other children are touchers – as they drift off to sleep, they fiddle with their mother's hair, or rhythmically stroke some skin.

# Tension in the family

Every year, thousands of children witness the break-up of their parents' relationship but this is only a small part of the problem. A great many more continue to live unhappily with parents who are geographically together but emotionally and behaviourally a million miles apart.

It is not just the alcoholics, the psychopaths and the violent who upset their children; it is also the thousands upon thousands of normal parents who bicker, nitpick, hold grudges, escalate events and make little effort to maintain their home as a happy and peaceful place.

## Tension stresses children

Don't fool yourself for a minute, you can never hide tension and unhappiness from children. You may keep your disputes and disagreements behind closed doors but the chill that comes with them will permeate to every corner of the home. Whether we like it or not, our adult problems soon become our children's problems.

Tension makes parents irritable, unreasonable, and emotionally tepid. Children, when they feel these vibes, may become insecure, demanding or just downright difficult. Most of this is quite unnecessary if only we adults could act more like adults and less like self-centred, inconsiderate toddlers.

Settling our disputes in an amicable way may not be as satisfying to our adult anger but it is important to the emotional wellbeing of our children. While parents have the right to fight, children have the right to be spared trauma.

# Break-ups: protecting the children

It is not the breakdown of a marriage that does the damage. Rather it is all the associated aggravation and hostility that upsets our children. Thankfully, not only are amicable settlements possible between divorcing partners but they are also very common. Remember:

■ The main priority is always the emotional wellbeing of our children.

■ Never underestimate the detrimental effect of stress and hostility on children. Parents may feel angry, but that's their problem, not the child's.

■ You can't stop the break-up but you can ensure that it is as amicable as possible.

■ Children need as little change as possible.

■ Children show they are upset by clinging close, acting out or withdrawing.

■ Children need to be told what is happening, in a way that is appropriate to their age.

■ Don't draw children into adult battles. They don't understand the rights and wrongs; all they know is that it hurts.

- Children need to know they will have two parents and both will continue to care for them. They should know where they will live. Where the non-custodial parent will live. And when they will see each other.

- Keep close to grandparents and any extended family who genuinely wish to support.

- You may divorce your partner, but your children do not want to divorce their grandparents. With break-ups children need the security of grandparents.

- Access must be encouraged and made easy. It's going to happen whether the parents make it enjoyable or a time of tension.

- Don't spy on or slander the other parent.

- When a child is out on access, it is up to the accessing parent what they do and whom they do it with. You can't prevent your child being cared for by a new partner.

# THIRTEEN

# Sibling Rivalry

Parents who have only one child rarely realise just how much their life will change when they have two. Two together are usually the best of friends but they can also be fierce rivals. Most behave best when alone and are at their worst when competing.

Young ones resent not being able to do things as well as their older brother or sister. They feel that others get privileges they don't. They compete for attention and object when they think they have got less, be it love or a serving of pudding. Little ones taunt older ones and older ones taunt the littlies.

This is what we call sibling rivalry and it is behind many an annoying display of bad behaviour. It is quite normal in toddlerhood, and probably will continue through to the age they leave home.

## Two toddlers – double trouble

When the Greens had just one toddler, I thought I knew all about children's behaviour. When we had two, I realised how little I knew. Two toddlers are never difficult when separated by a distance of at least a kilometre; it is when they come together that they set each other off.

The creative genius of such young people is always astonishing. A duet of toddlers can devise ways to get into mischief well beyond the imagination of any adult or child alone.

**All young animals love to squabble and fight. This builds up their bodily reflexes and muscles, while it drives their parents mad.**

When we talk of sibling rivalry in the toddler, the presentation depends very much on the child's age. The very young are keen to protect their home pitch from interfering intruders. Older toddlers have a different but equally difficult style – they squabble. The young behave badly when their toys are touched by brothers, sisters or visitors and they hate anyone monopolising their mum's attention. Older ones just bicker, bait and complain of inequality. This is a strange age where they can't bear to be apart but when together, they show their affection in a very odd way.

## True equality

We all know that each of our children must be treated with equal love, limits and discipline. We also know that this admirable goal is often out of touch with the reality of life in our own homes. The discipline and expectations may be equal but the children we discipline are not.

No matter how high our ideals are at the start, the quiet one may miss out while the difficult noisy one hijacks an unfair slice of the action. Time and attention may not be divided fairly but our love is still transmitted with complete equality.

Try hard to be totally fair, but when this is sabotaged by two children with dramatically different temperaments it may be necessary to tone down our expectations, steer round trouble and not force unwinnable issues.

# Fighting

Fighting between our young is one of those universal but irritating parts of family life. Over the years I have talked to hundreds of parents trying to find some foolproof peace-keeping methods but so far they remain elusive. However, I do have some suggestions that may help to secure an uneasy sort of truce.

■ Turn a deaf ear and a blind eye to as much squabbling as you can.

- When siblings start to spar, divert them onto something more innocent and interesting.

- Bundle squabbling children into another room or banish them out the back door. They can fight but they cannot expect an audience.

- It would take a team of detectives to find who started the fight. Don't waste your time. It is usually the one who protests loudest who is most guilty.

- At the first grunt don't rush in like the United Nations peace keepers. Children have to find their own equilibrium.

- It becomes a different matter when one child is being unfairly and continually victimised. Now firm action is needed.

- When we do intervene, it must be decisive, without debate and with 100 per cent firmness.

- When all else fails, separate the squabblers with a brief period of Time Out in different rooms.

The main mistake we parents make is to get drawn into our children's battles. If the moment they start you rush in like the army, grenades and guns at the ready, soon they will squabble just to see you in full action.

Few fights take place without an audience. If there is not an interested audience, most fights will fizzle out. When our children squabble it is best to either move away from the ringside, or move the ringside away.

If you are eventually forced to become involved, do so properly. Don't hold an enquiry into who fired the first shot as, at the height of any conflict, it is peace not recrimination that is needed.

Don't enter the squabble yourself. Pull rank, say 'that's it!' and leave them in no doubt that you are not going to take sides or tolerate any more. When this fails it is time for the warriors to be separated then banished for a while to their rooms.

# The toddler and the new baby

There is commonly a gap of about 1½ to 2½ years between our first and second child. This spacing means the unsuspecting baby is going to drop in on top of a self-centred toddler at the peak of his militancy.

From a 2-year-old's view, he thinks he is the most important person around. He likes having his mum's and dad's undivided attention. He doesn't understand the meaning of the word share and no-one asked his permission to bring that thing into the house.

Sometimes children may seem to regress when the new baby arrives home. They will suddenly start behaving like a baby themselves. They will want a bottle, want to be on mum's breast again and may even start talking like a baby. Children who have been toilet trained may start to wet their pants again. It's nothing to worry about, it will last for a while, then go away again.

**Be reassured that babies and toddlers come together well if parents make the right introductions.**

We do need to be careful, however. With the arrival of the new baby, the toddler discovers how sensitive and overprotective his mother has become. For some reason she cannot accept that a grubby, accident-prone 2-year-old should be allowed to manhandle her newborn piece of perfection.

When life becomes boring, all that is needed is for the toddler to walk a few paces and poke the baby. The result is quite dramatic, but even this effect can be surpassed by jumping on the infant or tipping up the pram.

It is important to protect but not overprotect the baby. If the toddler is scolded for going near the baby, who then receives cuddles and comfort, this is the surest way to sow the seeds of an unhealthy sort of sibling rivalry.

Within certain limits the toddler should be allowed to play with the new arrival and poke him just as long as he does not cause significant hurt. While all this is going on the parents must try to act nonchalant and keep off the stage. It is best to stand a short distance away and out of eyeshot of your toddler to watch that the baby suffers no harm.

## Making the right introductions

Life is much easier if we introduce toddlers to babies carefully and give attention to both in a way that appears to be equal. Here are some suggestions.

- When pregnant, talk to the toddler about a new brother or sister and how mum will need a little helper if she is to cope. Discuss possible names for the baby. Mention the impending arrival of all those dirty nappies. Toddlers can relate to this, as they are world experts on bodily functions.

- Visits to the post-natal ward should be a fun time with lots of fuss over the toddler and a few little presents on hand to sweeten the occasion.

- Visitors who come to see the baby must first fuss over and notice the toddler. After all, toddlers see themselves as the main attraction.

- Though tired and overprotective of the new infant, try hard to give the appearance of equal attention. This can be achieved by what I refer to as 'sidestream attention'. As you feed the baby, use the toddler as mother's little helper, talk or read a story.

- Of course mums are sensitive and highly protective of their newborn infants, but this must never be permitted to put a wedge between the toddler and baby. If you cuddle the baby and scold the toddler every time they come together, this is the surest way to create resentment and unhealthy rivalry.

- If handled well, most toddlers will accept their baby brother or sister without the slightest hiccup initially but when the baby is around the age of 6 months, there may be a backlash. At first new babies are seen as interesting animated dolls but at 6 months, when they sit up and start to do other clever things, they then become a great threat to the balance of power.

- Be reassured that most new babies and toddlers will come together well if parents are sensible.

# Are only children disadvantaged?

This can cut both ways, depending on how you look at it. In some ways only children are advantaged. They get more of their parents' time and tend to get more education.

On the other hand, they miss out on playing with peers and, as a result, often have rather more adult attitudes. They can be out of place in the company of adults or other children. This means that they may find it harder to settle down when they get to preschool.

But when you add it all up, I don't think there is any great disaster in being an only child. Parents shouldn't worry – the advantages and disadvantages balance themselves out.

# FOURTEEN

# Working Parents, Day care and Preschool

Mothers who have young children and go out to work are often censured, but no-one has yet shown that children of good, working parents are damaged or disadvantaged in any way. For an ever-increasing number, there is no choice – if there are not two wages the bills cannot be paid.

Working mums particularly feel guilty because they think they are short-changing their children. Although frequently blamed for their children's troubles, it is now apparent that the children of working mothers have no more problems than the children of mothers who remain at home. One recent study evaluated children's language development, academic achievement, self-esteem and behaviour problems. In comparison with children of mothers who did not work, no statistically significant difference was found in any of the measures.

It is increasingly clear that it is not the number of hours spent away from home that make the difference but:

- the quality of the child's day-care arrangements

- the quality of parent–child relationship

- Mum's emotional wellbeing

- extra attention given to the child when parents and child are together.

## Day care

Those lucky enough to be surrounded by family are fortunate indeed. Grandmas and grandpas are some of our most valuable and least utilised natural resources. If this help is not available, day care can be arranged (using either high quality approved centres or a local mother authorised to take in three or four children in her own home), but there are at present only half the places needed and even then they prove too expensive for many parents.

With a private arrangement, you must have complete confidence in the carer's ability so that you can relax when at work and concentrate on the job in hand. When choosing a care giver, watch how they relate to your little one. Do they talk, listen, play and share genuine parenting gentleness and care?

When the child is first left with a minder, enough time should be allowed so that this isn't done with a great rush and fuss. The child should be clearly told where you are going and when you will be back to pick him up. Despite the explanation, the young toddler will

**In Australia today, 51 per cent of mothers of under-5s are back in paid work.**

not understand and may shed copious tears on your departure. The minder should be left with a contact telephone number and told to telephone you if they have the slightest worry. This will help ensure a better standard of care for the child and some early warning for you if anything goes wrong.

Although most toddlers do well in the care of a good child minder, a few are immensely unhappy and never really settle. If this happens, the parents must ask themselves if separation is really necessary and if it might not be kinder to wait several more months before continuing. Of course in the modern world many parents are forced for a variety of good reasons to leave their child with a babysitter whether they like it or not.

## A fair deal for the child

Parents who work must make sure they give good attention to their child in the time that they are together. Work-tired parents often feel little enthusiasm to start washing, cleaning the house and cooking, let alone talking and playing with a toddler. But, however good day care is, it is only acceptable if accompanied by good night care and weekend care. Shopping, cooking and housework must not be allowed to consume all the parents' and child's time together, although if handled properly these can be a source of fun and education.

Working parents and a 'Home Beautiful' are not a compatible combination. Cleanliness, hygiene and relative tidiness are desirable but obsessive house pride is out. Family fun comes first. It is hard to communicate with a child over the roar of a vacuum cleaner and difficult to have a good, fun-filled romp around the house when obsessive parents resent the slightest disturbance to even a cushion.

## A fair deal for working mothers

Working mothers are often expected to do at least two full-time jobs, only one of which receives pay or thanks. It seems only fair that if children are planned and conceived together, then care should continue together. In the twenty-first century, there can be no place for a sleeping partner in a two-wage family. Fathers must wake up to this reality.

When two tired parents and an excited child get home each evening there must be a fair division of labour and the child must not miss out. Weekends can have one parent shopping, cleaning or taking the toddler to the pool or park, while the other irons and prepares for the week to come. If fathers can have a night out with the boys or go off to soccer training, mothers must be afforded the same opportunity.

An ever-increasing number of mothers with young children return to work and without help the stress will start to show.

# Preschool

Preschools take children from about 3 years old until school enrolment. The child stays at the centre, where all care and teaching is in the hands of the preschool staff. Preschool is a time for the child to enjoy and to develop a wide spectrum of skills needed for life and school. They provide an opportunity for gentle separation in a child who has previously been close, day and night, to his parents.

The best way to describe the activities of preschool is 'learning how to learn'. The child is taught basic skills necessary for life at school. These include sharing, mixing, sitting, settling, listening and sticking to a particular task. Many children find this immensely difficult at first but

**I think that preschool provides some of the best speech therapy available.**

the skilled, trained teachers know how to hold a child's waning interest and encourage him to sit and finish a task, bringing some structure and gentle discipline into the child's life.

The skilled teacher builds on the child's natural curiosity to develop an enthusiasm for learning and a quest for knowledge, as well as encouraging the child to both make and be a friend. Speech also accelerates at preschool, as all those busy little beings chatter among themselves.

The child is not the only one who benefits from preschool. If there is a younger child in the family, he will now receive some valuable one-to-one care, which he deserves without competition from the older child.

## Hints for starting preschool

Usually by the age of 3 years and certainly by 4 years our toddlers are ready for preschool. At such a young age there is however a great variation in each child's ability to separate. Here are some practical tips to help your toddler and you get through the first weeks:

■ In the months before, talk about preschool, visit, walk past and mentally prepare.

- Get them used to their new gear, the kindy bag, the lunch box, etc.

- Be sensible with clothes because toilet urgency is at its peak.

- The food you send should be simple, nutritious and easy to eat.

- Food should be packed in an easily opened lunch box with the child's name clearly marked.

- You don't have to compensate for your guilt about leaving your child by giving out unsuitable treats.

- Make sure that it is clear which packet is for little lunch and which is for the big lunch.

- On starting day set out in good time, don't rush and try not to transmit your uneasiness to the toddler.

- Go in with purpose, hang up the bag and take a tour of the premises. The toilets should be first stop as these will be much used in the year that follows.

- There may be a few wet pants. Make sure you put a spare pair of pants in the bag.

- Don't rush your departure on the first day. Sit and play and give them time to settle.

- When it is time to go, leave decisively.

- If you are worried about your child during the day, ring the preschool – they are used to it!

## When to graduate from preschool

Life is lived at such a pace there is no time to savour the present. From the moment of birth, some parents push their children on the fast track to independence. If the local law allows their child to start education at 4 years and 7 months, that's when they will begin.

But there is no need for such a rush: school enrolment is usually not compulsory until the age of 6 years. *Young children vary greatly in their social and emotional maturity.* Some are ripe for an early start, but others need more months to develop. If your child is eligible to start school young, look carefully at their social readiness. Discuss next year with their preschool teacher. They know how your child compares with the others who are preparing for school. When the teacher says no, take it seriously.

Many parents have no choice as, for them, school provides the only affordable form of child care. But if you have concerns and finances will support it, take the safe option and hold back. A late start will never do harm, but starting too soon can cause problems that don't go away.

# FIFTEEN

# Illness

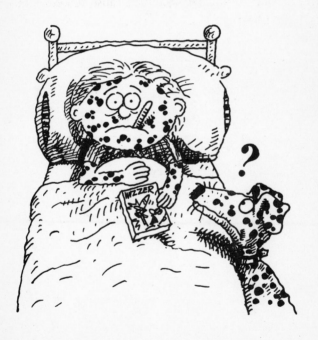

Hardly a day goes by without the toddler suffering from something – tonsillitis, an ear infection or the common cold. As part of growing up, the child goes through a whole series of illnesses, all quite common and in most cases nothing to be feared. This chapter is designed as a pointer to the parent but naturally if you are worried, take your child to a doctor.

## The common cold

Colds are caused not by one but by a number of viruses, which explains why one infection may follow straight after another, giving the impression of a non-stop nose run. As they are viruses, they do not respond to treatment with antibiotics but cure themselves, usually within four or five days. When the child first goes to day care or preschool, he is coughed over by a multitude of virus-splattering infants, and this is frequently his worst year for infections. Eventually some immunity is acquired, and the number of illnesses gradually

**Average toddlers will get up to nine colds each year, with six being about the usual number, which works out at about one every eight weeks.**

decreases each year until adulthood. Most of the natural immunity which a baby inherits from his mother is lost by the age of 6 months, and the first winter thereafter is often a prime one for colds.

Colds are spread by playmates and other people with whom the toddler comes into contact; they do not come from getting wet or playing out in the cold, whatever the myths may be.

There is no specific treatment for colds, although paracetamol (Panadol) preparations may make the child feel more comfortable.

## Tonsils

Tonsillitis is the specific infection of the tonsillar tissues at the back of the throat and their associated glands. The tonsils are not just red but 'angry' looking with flecks of pus. It is usually caused by bacteria and should be treated with antibiotics.

Tonsils are minute in the young toddler, reaching their peak size at about 7 years. Surgical removal of tonsils is rarely necessary in the toddler years. It may be considered if there are many recurrent infections or chronic infection. Size alone is not an indication for removal. Large tonsils do not cause feeding problems.

## Medicines: how to give them

It might be difficult to get a toddler to take medicine. If an unpleasant-tasting medicine has been prescribed once, ask if there is a more palatable alternative next time. Sometimes there are preparations that require fewer doses a day.

Most drugs can be given in liquid form to toddlers, preferably on a spoon and chased down by a favourite drink. Sometimes a plastic syringe is more effective. If capsules or tablets are given, the mouth should be moist before their introduction. Tablets slip down the throat with the greatest of ease when placed in a little ice-cream.

# Croup

This is a juvenile form of laryngitis, usually caused by a virus, which creates an infection in the region of the child's voice box (larynx). Antibiotics are usually no help. The child with croup makes a characteristic and often frightening 'crowing' noise when breathing in, accompanied by a cough like the sound of a sea lion. In its mild form, it can be easily treated at home with humidity.

A small minority of children can become quite seriously ill, and if their condition deteriorates rapidly or there is any other medical concern, seek help immediately.

## Asthma

Asthma affects about 20 per cent of all children. Despite the current media and medical interest in asthma, it is still inadequately treated. Its hallmark is a musical wheeze that comes from the depths of the lungs, mostly when breathing out. It may be induced by exercise and viral respiratory infections. It is often associated with periods of dry coughing in the middle of the night.

Most asthmatic children have the condition in a mild form, and they can live a completely normal, unrestricted life. Treatment uses certain medicines – relievers and preventers – to open up the air passages and they are best administered as inhalants through a spacer. These products are now extremely safe and highly effective, and they do not lose potency with continued use. Make sure the doctor has given you a step-by-step asthma action plan for intervention if needed. Allergy testing may be helpful for a small number of children.

Unfortunately a common cause of coughing in toddlers is exposure to passive smoke from adults.

# Ear problems

## Hearing loss

Most children who have severe hearing loss are now diagnosed between 6 and 9 months of age. However I have seen cases where it has remained undiagnosed until 18 months. If the child does not respond to quiet, unexpected noises, if his speech development is slow, or if there is the slightest doubt in the parents' minds, a proper hearing test should be arranged. Consider hearing loss if you talk comfortingly to a baby who is crying and he does not change the rhythm of crying to that of your speech. A child with normal hearing will respond when you walk into the room unnoticed and speak quietly. If the theme tune of *The Tweenies* is playing, a child with normal hearing will turn to the sound.

## Middle ear infection (otitis media)

Following a cold, a swim, or diving into a pool, bacteria may enter the middle ear and an infection can develop. The child becomes sick, irritable, has ear pain and partial hearing loss. On examination, the ear drum looks angry and red. As the infection is usually caused by bacteria, antibiotics are given, along with pain-killers, such as paracetamol (Panadol).

## Vomiting and diarrhoea

These are both extremely common in the toddler. When vomiting and diarrhoea are present together this often means an infection in the gut (gastroenteritis); if vomiting occurs alone, it may be due to an infection elsewhere, e.g. a middle ear infection. If your child is very sick, medical help should be sought. If the child is not too unwell, here are a few tips.

Children with acute gut infections need fluids, not solids. If there are going to be problems, it is through loss of water and salt. If vomiting and diarrhoea are caused by gastroenteritis, it is almost always of viral origin. They are not helped by antibiotics, which often have the side-effect of causing the diarrhoea to become worse.

Milk is best abandoned altogether. The correct treatment for vomiting is to give small amounts of clear fluids, frequently:

■ **Small** means no more than one whisky measure of fluid at a time.

- *Clear* means clear, not milk, not solids, not body-building protein, just fluid.

- *Frequently* means each quarter or half hour during the day. Set your timer. Although this may seem very little fluid, you can in fact administer 1.5 litres a day in this way.

I strongly recommend an oral electrolyte solution from the pharmacy such as Gastrolyte™ or Repalyte™. Some parents find it easier to present this solution as an ice block. If you don't have access to the chemist in the middle of the night, readily available everyday ingredients from the kitchen cupboard can be used to mix up a solution recommended by the World Health Organisation:

   1 litre cooled boiled water
   6 flat teaspoons sugar
   $^1/_2$ teaspoon salt

## Summary
- Vomiting in toddlers is common and may accompany any childhood illness, even the most trivial.

- When the child has considerable vomiting and diarrhoea, the cause is usually viral gastroenteritis, in which case the child does not need calorific foods, milk, chalk medicines, or antibiotics.

- He should be given only clear fluids, in small amounts, frequently.

- If the child looks sick, 'distant', dull-eyed, weak and passes little urine, or if you are at all worried, get medical help at once.

## Fevers

When the body is upset by an infection, whether it is a common cold or something more serious, the temperature will rise in response. The presence of a fever is merely an indication that the child is sick; the height of temperature is not an accurate barometer of the severity of the problem.

High temperature will upset the already unhappy child and make him feel more miserable. Also, some children with fevers are prone to fits. For both these reasons, young children with temperatures tend to be treated more vigorously than their adult counterparts.

A feverish child must be dressed sensibly, not wrapped

up in extra clothes and put into a bed heaped up with blankets. He should be given one of the commercial children's paracetamol preparations, as aspirin in young children is dangerous and should not be given.

Plunging the hot child into a bath filled with water straight from the Arctic is not only exceedingly cruel but also counterproductive. The proper procedure is to strip the child down to his pants and, if the temperature is still high, sponge him over gently with tepid, rather than cold, water. This gives a gentle, cooling effect and does not precipitate shivering or divert the blood away from the skin.

## Meningococcal infection

Meningococcus is one of the most feared infections of the moment. This has been increased by extensive media coverage. Out of the blue a child can embark on a devastating downhill course that may lead to death or disability. Despite this, it is one of the easiest bacteria to kill, responding to the most basic 1940s brand of penicillin.

The meningococcus bacterium is a relatively common fellow traveller in the community. Why it infects some people and misses the majority is unknown. It is an uncommon infection though cases have doubled in the past ten years. The bacterium enters the body, initially causing a mild illness with fever and often a fine rash. This moves on to septicaemia (blood infection) or meningitis (an infection of the tissue that covers the brain). Most children I have treated had both the septicaemia and meningitis. The presence of septicaemia is suspected in any extremely sick child with an almost-bruised-type skin rash that increases every minute. Meningitis is considered in the child with headache and a stiff neck.

A doctor can easily be caught out, seeing a vaguely sick child in the morning, giving reassurance, and sending them home. But some hours later the infection becomes all-consuming, with the child crashing onto the downhill course.

If any child looks sick and is dropping fast, this is the most urgent of urgent emergencies. The only way to prevent death and disability in meningococcus is a quick diagnosis, immediately followed by that first dose of life-saving antibiotic.

There are a number of different sorts of meningococcus. A vaccine effective against a dangerous strain (Men C) was introduced in the UK in late 1999. Meningococcal B vaccine is currently undergoing trials in New Zealand.

# The sick child: when to panic

I believe that most of the clues in 'the sick child' are in the eyes and the child's alertness. Seek medical attention when a child:

- is pale, sweaty and looks anxious

- is passing little urine, has a dry mouth, has a lack of elasticity in the skin and has sunken eyes

- is panting, over breathing or has a deep rattling breath

- has a stiff neck which is painful to move or bend.

When mum is worried, I worry. When mum and grandma are worried, I worry a lot!

# Home Safety Checklist

## Home environment

- Do you have a safety switch to prevent electrocution?

- Can your hot water system be turned down to 50 degrees Celsius to prevent scalds?

- Do you have a smoke detector located outside each bedroom area?

- Are safety plugs fitted in spare power points?

- Do you have a fence that restricts access to your driveway and the street?

## Kitchen

- Do your appliances have short cords that do not dangle over the kitchen bench?

- Do you use the back hot plates and turn pot handles around to prevent pots being pulled from the hot plates?

- Are knives and other sharp objects stored out of reach of children?

- Are cleaning products, chemicals and medications stored in a locked cupboard at least 1.5 metres above the ground?

- Do you have a fire blanket within reach of your stove?

- Can you restrict access to the kitchen?

## Bathroom

- Does the bath have non-slip mats or hand rails?

- Are medicines and sharp objects kept in a locked cupboard out of reach of children?

- Are any electricals (i.e. hairdryers, electric shavers) stored safely and away from water when not in use?

- Is the bath water temperature always 'tested' before putting the child in the bath?

- Are hot water taps unable to be operated by small children?

## Laundry

■ Are cleaning products, bleaches and detergents stored out of reach, in a child-resistant cupboard?

■ Is the nappy bucket used with a lid on and kept out of reach of children?

■ Can you restrict access to the laundry?

## Living areas

■ Is the furniture located safely (e.g. away from windows)?

■ Are sharp edges on tables and furniture covered?

■ Are blind and curtain cords out of reach?

■ Are glass doors protected by safety film, colourful stickers or made of safety glass?

■ Is alcohol stored in a child-resistant cupboard?

■ Are toys kept away from the main walkway?

■ Are rugs and mats secure to prevent a fall?

■ Are there any low-level tables that dangerous items could be placed on (e.g. watch batteries, tea and coffee, peanuts)?

## Child's bedroom

■ Is the space between vertical cot railings between 50 mm and 85 mm wide?

■ Are toys suitable for the child's age?

■ Is the furniture located safely (i.e. not near electrical switches, windows or ceiling fans)?

## Garden shed/outdoors

■ Can your garden shed be locked at all times?

■ Are pesticides, paints and other poisons stored in tightly covered, labelled, original containers out of reach of children?

■ Check that outdoor play equipment is not damaged or potentially dangerous.

■ Does your pool have a fence at least 1.2 m high around all four sides of the pool, that cannot be climbed by children and has a self-closing, self-latching gate?

(Courtesy, The Children's Hospital, Westmead, Sydney.)

*Also available from Vermilion by Dr Christopher Green*

# New Toddler Taming
## A Parents' Guide to the First Four Years

Over 1 million copies sold!

Revised and updated for the twenty-first century, *New Toddler Taming* offers friendly, practical advice for a new generation of parents with children at the challenging stage of toddlerdom.

With today's parents increasingly pressed for time, yet under pressure to succeed both at work and at home, Dr Green's reassuring message is to remember that you are normal and not alone. The key to effective parenting, he says, is knowing what to expect and having the self-confidence to see the various stages through.

Based on over twenty-five years' experience, Dr Green's methods will help you to enjoy the toddler years. With his trademark humour and common sense he demystifies child care and brings the fun back into parenting. *New Toddler Taming* includes:

- sleep solutions that really work
- successful potty training
- the very latest on healthy eating

- discipline – how to make life easier for yourself
- dealing with trantrums
- surviving sole-parenting, being a working parent and much more!

### *From the author*

I used to think I was a real expert on child care, but that was before I had children of my own. When my boisterous boys arrived, I discovered how little I knew, and how out of touch and impractical was the vast majority of child care information available.

That was 25 years ago, and from there I set out to find some more appropriate ways of managing and enjoying our young. I started by bouncing my own amateur ideas off parents I saw each day in my practice. Some returned a week later, amazed with the success of my suggestions, while others told me I was crazy.

As the months and years went by, the ineffective techniques were dumped, while the good ones were built on, refined and tested by the hundreds of parents I saw. After eight years, I realised that I had been given a unique education thanks to the thousands of parents who showed me the realities of child care. Thus *Toddler Taming* was born.

The *Toddler Taming* message in this new edition is still

the same. The important things in child care will always remain: love, consistency, example, tension-free homes and above all sensible expectations.

It's all too easy to believe that child care is a complex science, when in fact it is very natural. Parents have been doing it well for years without authors like me interfering. Time with our children passes all too quickly. Life is not a video, you can't press the rewind button to view it again.

Children are fun – enjoy them now!

*Dr Christopher Green, 2001*

# Beyond Toddlerdom

## Keeping five- to twelve-year-olds on the rails

The sequel that every parent has been waiting for . . .

*Beyond Toddlerdom* is for all parents in need of calm and wise advice on parenting the 5–12 age group. Written in his usual humourous, practical and down-to-earth style, Dr Christopher Green takes full account of all the physical, psychological and sociological influences that are of importance during this time – and helps parents to make appropriate decisions about everything from friends and homework to sibling rivalry and positive discipline.

### *From the author*

*Toddler Taming* was practical, reassuring and based on reality. What's more, it could make mums laugh. After all, you can smile about toddlers because you know that most of their odd little behaviours will disappear when their brain discovers sense at the age of three years.

But five- to twelve-year-olds are much more complicated, which made *Beyond Toddlerdom* a lot harder to write. These children are influenced by school, their friends, their families and their abilities, and their problems can easily deepen rather than disappear.

*Beyond Toddlerdom* looks at how primary school-age children feel, think and behave. The emphasis is on behaviour, with the aim of keeping parents close and in love with their children, so homes need never become a war zone.

I learnt the ideas you will read in this book from the thousands of parents and children I have attempted to help every day in my work. But I don't pretend to have all the answers: even after twenty-five years I still struggle to find ways to help some families I meet.

Hopefully, though, you will find lots of useful advice here. To help find what you're looking for easily and quickly, *Beyond Toddlerdom* contains a clear index and plenty of tables that set out the main points.

Once I asked a mum how things were going. She said, 'It's like this, Doctor. Before we met you we were riding on a roller coaster completely out of control. Now we're still on a roller coaster but it's finally on the rails.'

This book is about keeping relationships between parents and children strong and happy. It's also about keeping children on the rails. I can't promise a smooth ride, but I hope I can help you avoid some of the bumps.

*Dr Christopher Green, January 2000*

# AVAILABLE FROM VERMILION

☐ New Toddler Taming    0091875285    £12.99
☐ Beyond Toddlerdom    0091816246    £9.99
☐ Understanding ADHD    0091817005    £9.99

## FREE POST AND PACKING
Overseas customers allow £2.00 per paperback

## ORDER:

By phone: 01624 677237

By post: Random House Books
c/o Bookpost
PO Box 29
Douglas
Isle of Man, IM99 1BQ

By fax: 01624 670923

By email: bookshop@enterprise.net

Cheques (payable to Bookpost) and credit cards accepted

Prices and availability subject to change without notice.
Allow 28 days for delivery.
When placing your order, please mention if you do not wish to receive
any additional information

**www.randomhouse.co.uk**